An Introduction t
Desktop Publishing

Free Catalogue

If you would like, free of charge, a complete catalogue of our entire range of Radio, Electronics and Computer books, then please send a stamped addressed envelope to:—

An Introduction to Desktop Publishing

by
R.A. & J.W. Penfold

BERNARD BABANI (publishing) LTD
THE GRAMPIANS
SHEPHERDS BUSH ROAD
LONDON W6 7NF
ENGLAND

Please Note

First Published – June 1991

British Library Cataloguing in Publication Data
Penfold, R. A.
An introduction to desktop publishing.
1. Desktop publishing
I. Title II. Penfold, J. W.
070.50285416

ISBN 0 85934 214 X

Printed and Bound by The Guernsey Press Co. Ltd, Channel Islands

Preface

Desktop publishing (d.t.p.) is a relatively recently introduced application for microcomputers, and it has rapidly become one of the most popular uses for both home and business computer systems. Although at one stage it was widely predicted that computers would result in the so-called "paperless office", this does not seem to be an immediate prospect. Computers seem to be mainly used for producing documents and drawings reproduced on paper, and have probably resulted in more paper being used rather than less! Desktop publishing is a good example of how computers have been used to update a traditional task, with the final result being much the same as using the traditional methods, but with the speed of production being greatly increased. In most cases the production costs are substantially reduced. Although the "paperless office" may have failed to materialise, computers running applications such as desktop publishing have nevertheless revolutionised most aspects of office work.

Although desktop publishing seems to have become mainly associated with the production of business reports and similar material, it is something which has much wider application than this. It can be used for anything from the production of circulars advertising a jumble sale through to the preparation of large and fully illustrated books. This type of software is probably run on just as many home computers as office systems.

Probably the main advantage of desktop publishing for many users is that it enables well laid out documents to be produced without first having to spend large amounts of time learning a range of skills. Using a desktop publishing system is not a skill-free task, but it something that can be learned relatively quickly and easily. You can check page layouts on the screen of the monitor, and make any necessary adjustments with minimal difficulty before printing out the finished product. With some types of publication the program can be set up so that much of the page layout process is automatic, and the finished documents are produced with little manual intervention.

This book teaches you the basic methods used in desktop publishing, and explains the inevitable terminology (which is a mixture of computing and traditional publishing jargon). It covers various items of hardware, giving advice on their suitability for use in desktop publishing. Some advice on page layouts and styles is also provided. It is assumed that you know how to switch on your computer, run programs, and that you are familiar with a few basic computing terms. Otherwise, no previous computing or publishing experience is assumed.

R.A. & J.W. Penfold

Trademark Acknowledgements

MS-DOS and **Windows** are registered trademarks of Microsoft Inc.

IBM, PC XT, PC AT, and **PC-DOS** are registered trademarks of IBM Corporation.

GEM and **GEM ArtLine** are registered trademarks of Digital Research Inc.

Amstrad is a registered trademark of Amstrad Consumer Electronics plc

UNIX is a registered trademark of AT & T.

Apple, Macintosh and **LaserWriter** are registered trademarks of Apple Corporation.

Adobe and **PostScript** are registered trademarks of Adobe Inc.

Bitstream Fontware is a registered trademark of Bitstream Inc.

Timeworks Desktop Publisher, Timeworks DTP Lite, and **Typografica** are registered trademarks of GST Software Ltd.

Xerox Ventura Publisher is a registered trademark of Rank Xerox plc.

Aldus Pagemaker is a registered trademark of Aldus Inc.

Atari and **Atari ST** are registered trademarks of Atari Corporation.

Amiga is a registered trademark of Commodore Business Machines Ltd.

Archimedes is a registered trademark of Acorn Computers Ltd.

ITC Avant Garde, Dingbats, ITC Bookman and **ITC Zapf Chancery** are registered trademarks of International Typeface Corporation.

PaintJet, HPGL, DeskJet and **LaserJet** are registered trademarks of the Hewlett-Packard Company.

Corel Draw! is a registered trademark of Corel Systems Corporation.

Hercules is a registered trademark of Hercules Computer Technology.

WordPerfect is a registered trademark of the Wordperfect Corporation.

Lotus 1-2-3 is a registered trademark of Lotus Development Corporation.

Harvard Graphics is a registered trademark of Software Publishing Corporation.

AutoCAD is a registered trademark of Autodesk Inc.

Finesse is a registered trademark of AMS Ltd.

Contents

Page

Chapter 1
D.T.P. SOFTWARE

In terms of the facilities offered, and the method of use, there are considerable variations from one d.t.p. (desktop publishing) program to another. On the other hand, there are features and methods of working that are common to many d.t.p. programs. In this chapter we will consider some of the more common and important d.t.p. features, together with the basic ways in which these programs operate. This chapter is not intended as a tutorial to make you an expert at using every d.t.p. program. It would be totally impractical to provide such guidance, and there is no substitute for "hands-on" experience with your chosen d.t.p. program. Desktop publishing programs are mostly pretty complex pieces of software, and some studying of the manual plus some experimentation with the program will certainly be needed before your d.t.p. program is properly mastered.

Although detailed guidance on the use of particular d.t.p. programs can not be provided here, general principles can be explained. This should first aid the selection of a d.t.p. program that is suitable for your requirements, and secondly it should make it much easier to get to grips with the selected program.

Basics

The basic function of a d.t.p. program is to take some text, or some text and graphics, and to produce properly made up pages from them. Obviously text can be entered into a word processor and printed out, and with some word processors it is even possible to add graphics (diagrams, charts, etc.) into the text. Even the most powerful of word processors fall short of true d.t.p. standards though. With a d.t.p. program the pages can have multiple columns if desired, text can be as large or as small as you like (within reason), and a large number of text fonts and styles are available. A wordprocessor may well provide proportionally spaced text, but d.t.p. software should provide manual and automatic kerning (these terms are explained in detail later on). In fact with any reasonably good d.t.p. software you can make up pages of the type found in books, magazines, newspapers, etc. The limits are likely to be set more by your imagination than the limitations of the d.t.p. software.

Virtually all d.t.p. programs are designed to handle existing text files or graphics files stored on computer disks, rather than to have the text and graphics produced using the d.t.p. software itself. It is usually possible to type text into these programs, and in some cases there is some drawing capability. However, they do not provide facilities which compare with those of word processors or graphics programs. Entering text and graphics tends to be relatively slow and cumbersome. Editing facilities for both text and graphics are normally very limited.

The ability to enter and edit text is there mainly as a means of making corrections or minor alterations to the text once it has been loaded into the program, and not as the primary means of entering text. Similarly, the basic graphics facilities are only intended as a means of producing very simple diagrams, adding frames around imported graphics, and this type of thing. Any remotely complicated drawings normally have to be produced using a proper graphics program, and then loaded into the d.t.p. program.

Obviously it will not normally be sufficient to have just the d.t.p. software. It will need to be backed up by a word processor or text editor, and possibly one or more drawing programs. The latter will not be discussed here, as this topic is discussed in detail in a separate chapter. In theory, if you are making up pages using text supplied by other people on computer disks, you do not need a word processor or text editor. In reality you are likely to need one of these for producing odd pieces of text, and a simple text editor should be regarded as a minimum requirement.

Some computers are supplied complete with some form of text editor, or possibly even a sophisticated word processor. The software supplied with the computer might be all that you need, but most of the text editors that are included in the software bundled with computers are pretty basic, and not the most usable of programs. A low cost word processor or text editor is likely to be more practical. It is possible to obtain suitable public domain programs for many computers, and the cost of these is just a few pounds (i.e. the cost of the disk plus a small copying fee, etc.). The difference between a word processor and a text editor incidentally, is that a word processor has facilities for organising the text into pages and printing it out. A text editor either lacks these facilities, or only has very limited pagination and printing facilities.

In the current context, all that is needed is a program that permits the text to be entered into the computer, edited as necessary, and then stored on a computer disk. A text editor is therefore quite adequate for most purposes. If you are going to produce long articles, books, or any large pieces of text, then a good quality word processor will almost certainly prove to be well worth the cost. A program of this type should make it as easy as possible to enter and edit large chunks of text.

A point to keep in mind is that the word processor or text editor must be capable of generating text files that can be loaded into the d.t.p. program. Most computers handle text in the form of standard code numbers, and this system of coding is known as ASCII (American Standard Code for Information Interchange, and normally pronounced something like "asskey"). Any d.t.p. program should be capable of reading in text in this basic ASCII form. Most text editors produce text in this form as standard, and most word processors can be made to produce ASCII text files.

With word processors there may be limitations on the way in which text can be formatted when producing ASCII files, but as we shall see shortly, this does not really matter. Formatting the text in the required manner using the word processor or the text editor is not normally necessary, and is unlikely to be the best way of doing things anyway.

Word processors sometimes save text to disk as simple ASCII files, but it is more normal for them to be saved as ASCII files plus some special formatting codes. In some cases the text and formatting instructions are all coded in a fashion that is unique to the particular word processor concerned. In either case, these can not be read into a d.t.p. program unless it has a facility specifically for reading in files produced by the word processor in question. It is not uncommon for d.t.p. programs to be able to read files in some common word processor formats. The d.t.p. program will usually respond to some basic formatting commands, and if a line of text is centred using the word processor, it will probably remain centred once it has been loaded into the d.t.p. program. This is not invariably the case though, and the d.t.p. program might simply strip off all the formatting commands, leaving what is essentially just a basic unformatted ASCII file.

Embedded Commands

Having loaded some text into a d.t.p. program, it is necessary to have some means of laying out the pages in the required manner. In fact this process does not necessarily start once the text has been loaded into the d.t.p. program, and can start at the word processor or text editor stage. As we have already seen, simple formatting commands used when preparing the text may be carried on into the d.t.p. program. This method only gives very limited capabilities though, and is of equally limited practical value.

A system used by some d.t.p. programs is to permit the use of embedded commands within the imported text. This permits great control over the finished document, enabling a full range of formatting commands to be used, text fonts, styles and sizes to be selected, etc. The exact manner in which this system is implemented varies from one d.t.p. program to another, but it generally works along the lines of using something like a couple of code letters to select the required command, possibly with some figures to provide additional information. As a couple of examples, the letters "CE" could be used to indicate that a line of text (a headline perhaps) should be centred in its column, or the code "FT15" could be used to indicate a change to font number 15. With a system of this type it is possible to control the format of the text before it ever reaches the d.t.p. program.

There is an obvious problem with this method of doing things in that the d.t.p. program must be able to distinguish between the text and the formatting commands. This is normally achieved by including a little used character as part of each embedded command. Most computer keyboards include several of these unusual characters, such as |, \, ¬, and ~, which can be used for this type of thing. These characters are not normally used in plain text, and there is little risk of a piece of text being mistaken for an embedded command. There is a slight risk of the character in question turning up in specialised material, such as scientific papers, d.t.p. book manuscripts, etc., but in these cases it must be omitted from the text initially. It can probably be added safely later, once the text has been loaded into the d.t.p. program and formatted.

A slightly different approach to the problem is to use something like a space and a fullstop at the start of each embedded command (e.g. " .CE"). This is something that would not normally occur in plain text. At the end of a sentence you would normally have some text characters followed by a fullstop and a space, but not the inverse of this. The advantage of such a system is that it does not put any text characters, even little used ones, "off limits".

Obviously with any system of this type there is a slight risk of text being interpreted as an embedded command. However, in practice this is not a major problem, and for the vast majority of users it is something that will never occur. If it should happen, it is likely to be as a result of an error when entering the text, rather than by the system being fooled.

D.T.P. Formatting

Embedded commands are not usually the sole method of formatting text. In order to get the page layouts looking just right it is normally necessary to resort to at least a small amount of editing in the d.t.p. program. I suppose that it would be possible to have a d.t.p. program that simply took in a word processor file with embedded commands, and then produced the hard copy from this.

The drawback of this system is that you would not see each page until it was printed out. Any changes would have to be implemented by going back to the original word processor file, seeking out the appropriate embedded commands, and making the appropriate alterations. Even a few small changes could result in every page having to be reprinted. Remember that changes to one page can have a knock-on effect which results in changes to every subsequent page. Using embedded commands as the only method of controlling the page layout, etc., would therefore be a rather slow and inconvenient way of handling things. Also, there are some aspects of page design which are more easily handled in the d.t.p. program than by using embedded commands.

It is normal for d.t.p. programs to give full control over the layout, fonts used, text size, etc., from within the program itself, even if embedded commands are supported. It is only fair to point out that by no means all d.t.p. programs do actually support embedded commands. Where embedded commands are implemented, it is probably quicker if they are used for some basic formatting of the documents. This will not always be possible, and it is something that is unlikely to be practical if you are making up documents from disk files received from a number of different sources. You might be able to get the co-operation of those who supply the disk files, but being realistic about it, this approach will probably not be practical. Many d.t.p. users do not prefer this method of working anyway. This is a matter of personal preference, and where a program offers different means of achieving the same thing it is always a good idea to try them all out to see which one suits you best.

When text is loaded into a d.t.p. program, the display normally shows the first page of text. We are assuming here that the program is one that can handle multi-page documents, which most of them can. It is only fair to point out that there are a few simple d.t.p. programs which are strictly one page at a time types, unsuitable for large documents. These are used in much the same way as the multi-page d.t.p. programs, but they must either be fed with no more text than they can handle in a single page, or they will simply clip off any text which will not fit onto the first (and only) page.

Unless the display is a very high resolution type, it will not be possible to see both the whole page, and an accurate representation of the page on a letter by letter basis. There is invariably a solution to this problem in the form of pan and zoom facilities. These provide a detailed view of part of the page, and enable the viewing "window" to be moved around the page so that any desired part can be examined. The vast majority of programs provide a WYSIWYG (what you see is what you get) display, which simply means that the screen display is an accurate representation of the equivalent printed page, or is as close as the display can get to this at any rate. The better the display quality, the more accurate the representation of the page should be. Figure 1.1 shows a zoomed view of a page, while Figure 1.2 shows the full view of the same page.

At this stage, any formatting commands carried through from the word processor, or demanded by embedded commands, should be shown on the display. Otherwise there will just be a screenful of raw text, with no variations in font, text size, etc. To format the text in the desired manner it is largely a matter of indicating pieces ("blocks") of text that must be treated in some way. The method of selecting text and the required change varies from program to program, but these days most d.t.p. programs make heavy use of a mouse and pop-down menus. In most cases the commands can be selected via the keyboard using one or two key presses. The menus provide an easy means of learning to use the program initially, but can be a bit slow and frustrating for the experienced user. The keyboard commands then offer a quicker means of controlling the program, if you are prepared to learn all the command codes.

As a typical example of how text might be formatted in the desired manner, the first task would probably be to select the desired block of text. To do this the cursor is moved to the beginning of the

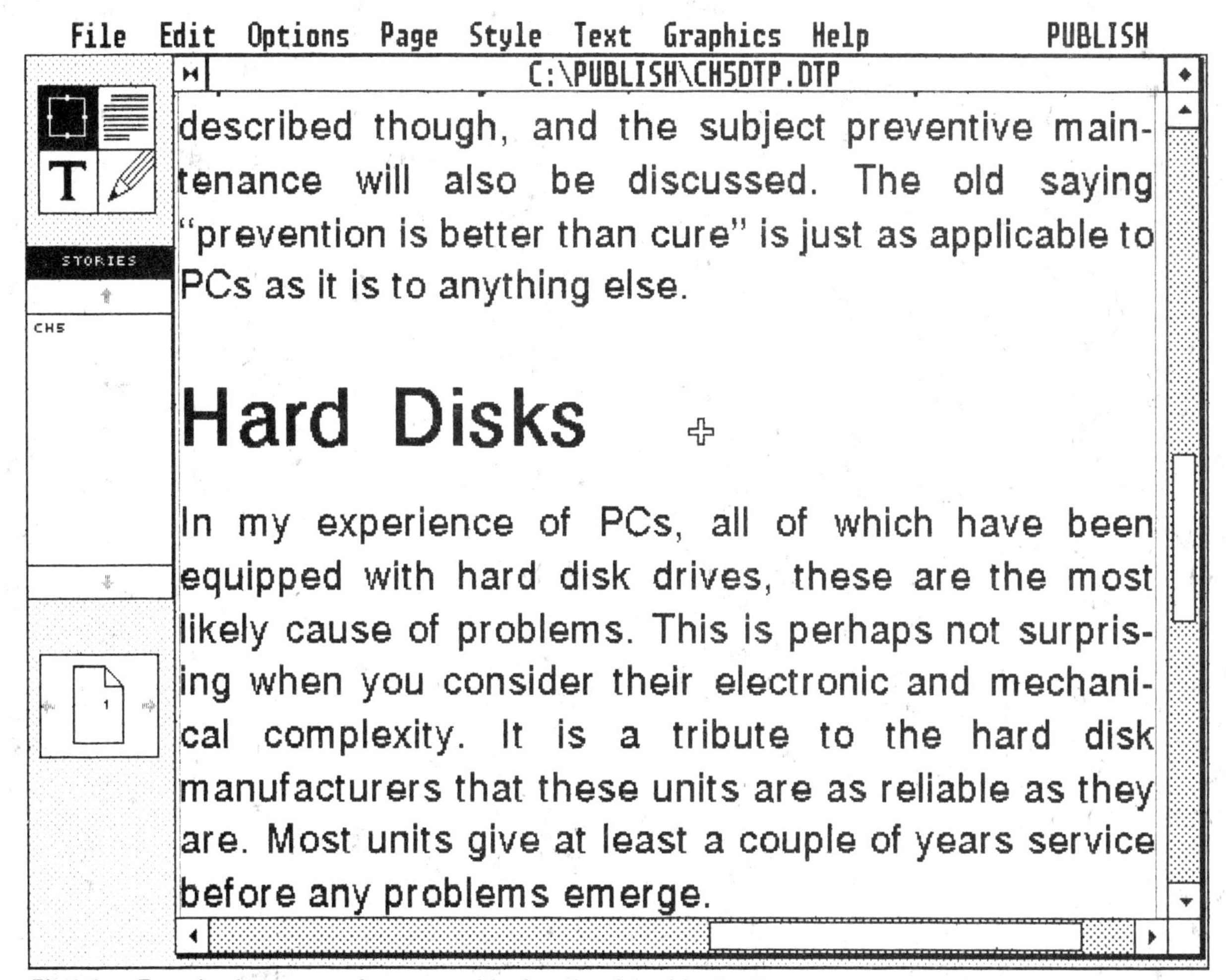

Fig.1.1 Zooming in on part of a page enables it to be viewed in detail

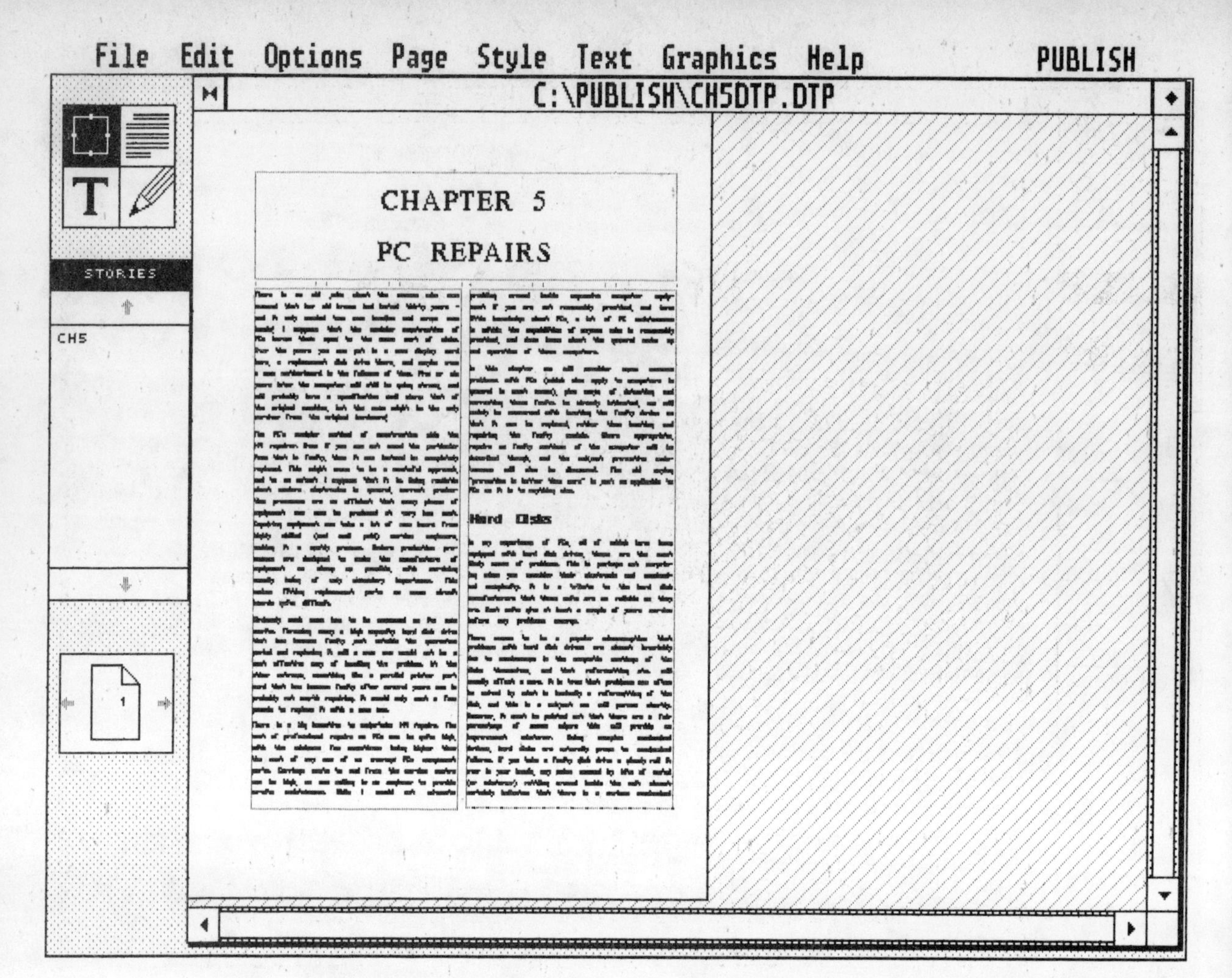

Fig. 1.2 With most d.t.p. systems the full page view shows no detail, but does give a good impression of how the printed-out page will look

text that is to be processed and a button on the mouse is depressed. Then the cursor is moved to the end of the block of text, and the button is released. The selected block of text will be marked on the screen in some way, so you can see that you have selected the right text, or that a mistake has been made and a fresh attempt is required. There may simply be marks left at the beginning and end of the block, but more usually it would be shown in inverse video or in a different colour to the rest of the text (Figure 1.3).

Next the required change to the text is selected. Suppose that the block of text that has been selected is actually a headline. This will need to be larger than the main text, and will probably need to be in a different font as well. You would therefore select the font command, select the desired font from a list that appears on the screen, and the text would then change to the new font. Then the text size command would be issued, and the desired text size would be selected. The line of text would then change to the new, larger size. With the text increased in size, it will obviously take up more space on the page. This is all handled by the d.t.p. program though, and the page is automatically adjusted to accommodate the larger text. This means that the text at the end of the page will be removed, and placed at the beginning of the next page. This will have a knock-on effect that will necessitate changes to all the subsequent pages, but the d.t.p. program will handle this automatically.

Having processed the headline satisfactorily, you would then move on to the main text, selecting the required font and text size again. Then sub-headings could be selected, and perhaps changed to a slightly larger text size and centred within their columns. In this way the text can quickly and easily be formatted in the desired fashion, soon leaving you with the first page ready to print out.

Global Formatting

So far we have only considered the formatting of text in terms of such things as the text fonts and sizes used, whether or not lines are centred, and this type of thing. There is also the overall page layout to consider (the number of columns, the gap between them, how close the text is taken to the foot of the page, etc.). With any d.t.p. program there will be a default setup, with a certain number of columns, a certain gap at the foot of the page, a "standard" font which is used for text when it is first loaded,

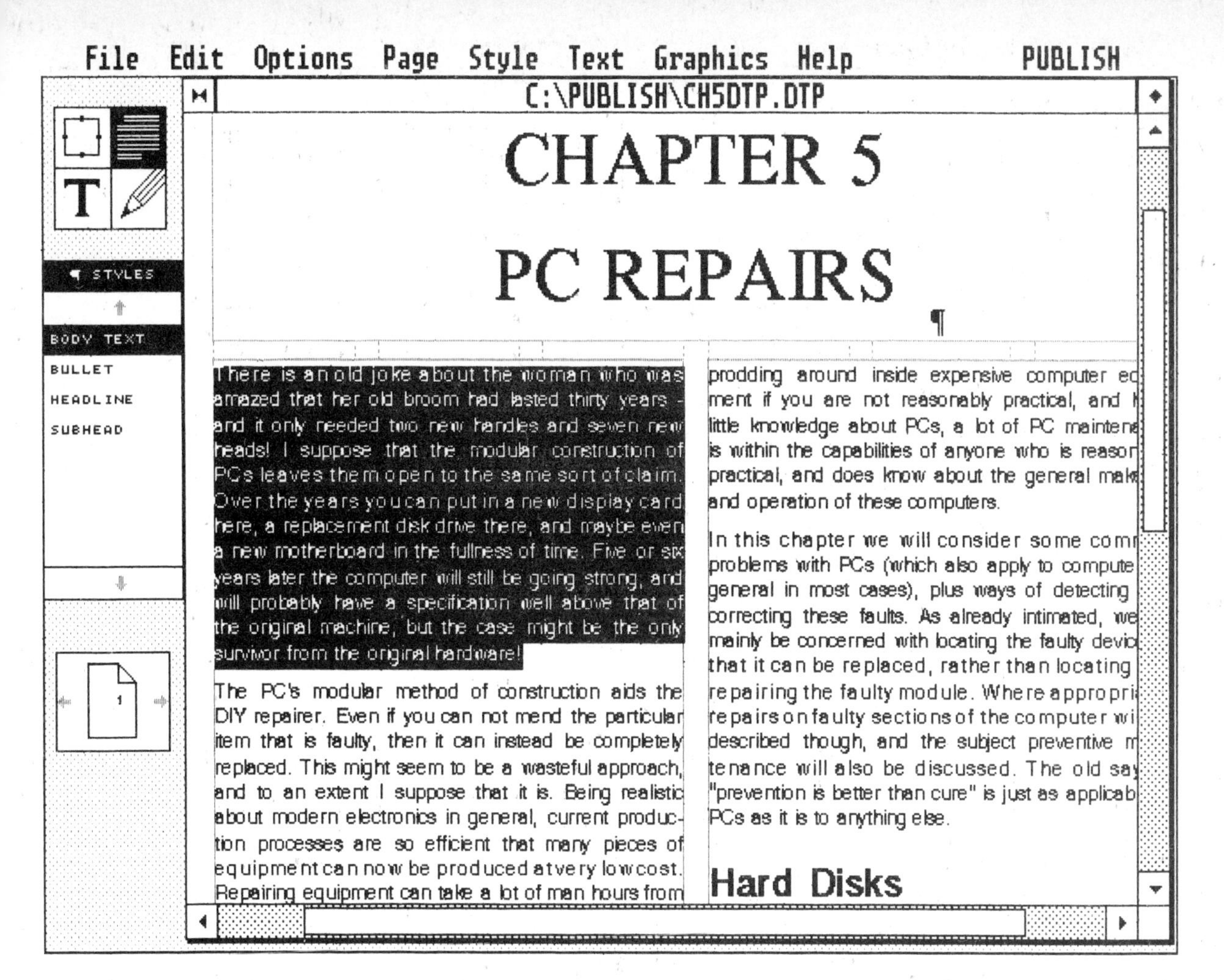

Fig. 1.3 *The block of text that has been selected for editing is shown in inverse video*

and so on. There are usually some on-screen marks to show the columns, and where loaded text will flow onto the page.

There is some ability to change all this in any d.t.p. program, but just how much flexibility is available is something that is entirely dependent on the particular program used. This is one respect in which the more expensive programs are usually very much better than the budget ones. With the more simple programs there are a few preset page sizes, plus a few standard page layouts, and you have to select the one which best suits your needs. With the most sophisticated d.t.p. programs you can select any page size within certain maximum and minimum limits, and exercise considerable control over the number of columns, the column width, the amount of empty space at the top and bottom of the page, etc.

With the traditional page make-up process, the text is in the form of galley proofs, which have the text printed in the right fonts, sizes, etc., and with the right column width, but in one long column. Any photographs, drawings, etc., are printed actual size, as they must appear in the final document. The page make-up artist then cuts up the text into pieces which are pasted onto page layout sheets, together with any drawings and photographs. The adhesive used is normally a non-drying type so that items can easily be moved around. The layout sheets are marked with column markers and other marks to aid the artist in getting things accurately positioned.

Some d.t.p. programs permit things to be done in a fashion which is analogous to this traditional page make-up method. This is not a method that can be recommended for newcomers to making up pages though. It is something that is included primarily for those who are very experienced at this sort of thing. In particular, it is aimed at those who have been making up pages using the traditional paste-up method, and who wish to change over to d.t.p.

The more normal approach is to first select or design the basic page layout, including such things as the number of columns, gap at the bottom of each page, the position of page numbers, and any headings to be included at the top of each page. The text is then loaded, and will flow into the columns. As explained previously, any formatting of the text that results in it expanding, such as changing headings to a larger text size, results in the text being automatically shuffled around to suit the new scheme of things. If you should change your mind and change the headings back to a smaller size, then the text will again be shuffled to fit the revised scheme. This is much easier and quicker than moving things around yourself.

Frames

This automatic adjustment of the text will normally take place when any significant changes are made to a page. If you add or delete any text for example, text will be moved down the page to make way for the new text, or the gap will be filled up where some text was removed. Most d.t.p. programs permit graphics to be imported into documents, or you can reserve areas on pages which are left blank so that photographs or drawings can be pasted onto the printout. If areas are reserved before the text is imported, when the text is loaded it will automatically flow around the areas reserved for graphics. In effect you are creating "no-go" areas for the text.

With most d.t.p. programs it is possible to alter the sizes of graphics frames, and the text will again be adjusted to fit the new layout. Usually it is also possible to add graphics frames after the text has been loaded, with the text once more being reformatted to suit the altered page layout. If a graphics frame is moved, the text is automatically shuffled around to suit the frame's new position. This automatic reformatting, together with a WYSIWYG display, makes it easy to get page layouts looking right, and looking right at the first attempt. Repeatedly printing out pages, making alterations and reprinting them, is a very slow and costly method of working. With a good d.t.p. program you can produce page layouts quickly, and will need to undertake minimal reworking of documents.

With many d.t.p. programs you are restricted to having graphics in rectangular frames, with the text being kept off these areas altogether. Some d.t.p. programs have a slightly different approach, where the loaded drawing itself is the "no-go" area, rather than the frame into which it is loaded. This may seem to make no difference, but the point to keep in mind here is that a drawing might not fill the frame into which it is loaded. There may be blank areas of background, and quite large areas at that. If the text is repelled by the drawing rather than by the graphics frame, the text is free to flow into these blank areas in the background. The text will therefore flow around the outline of the drawing, giving what is quite a neat effect if it is used sensibly. Like many of the advanced facilities in d.t.p. programs, it is not a good idea to use it simply because it is there. Flowing text around drawings is not appropriate for many types of technical publications for example.

With d.t.p. programs which do not have a facility of this type it is sometimes possible to get much the same effect. First text is loaded into the frame, but the frame is not made a "no-go" area for the text. Several graphics frames are then created, and made "no-go" areas, so that they keep the text off the appropriate areas of the drawing. This is a less convenient way of handling things, but it gives more control over where the text goes. With some automatic flow-around facilities you might find that the text gets closer to the drawings than you would really like. You will often find that with d.t.p. programs there are indirect means of getting special effects even if there is no proper facility provided. It pays to read the manual carefully, and to give some thought to methods of using the available facilities.

It is perhaps worth mentioning that there are text frames as well as graphics frames. Like a graphics frame, a text type repels the main text and produces a blank area on the screen. Instead of loading a drawing into this area, it is loaded with a small piece of text. This may seem a bit pointless, but with some types of publication, particularly technical types, it is quite common to have these text boxes to carry detailed explanations of points raised in the main text. Without a text frame capability it could be quite difficult to handle these text boxes. Not all d.t.p. programs have this facility, but many can now handle this type of thing, although not necessarily in an entirely straightforward manner.

Much d.t.p. work involves producing numerous documents that are all laid out very much along the same lines. In some cases it might be necessary to produce documents using several standard formats. Most up-market d.t.p. programs have some form of "style sheet" facility that enables the program to be tailored to suit one or more of these standard formats. The exact way in which this facility functions varies from program to program, but in most cases it is possible to produce finished documents largely automatically. With some embedded commands in the text file, and the right style sheet selected, the loaded text is given the right fonts and styles, flows into the required column format, and so on.

Obviously there will often be the need for some variation from one document to another, and it might not always be possible to produce finished documents without resorting to some manual editing. Using style sheets does not impede the program's editing facilities, so that any required customisation of documents can be carried out swiftly and easily.

Terminology

Like just about any aspect of computing, with d.t.p. programs you are likely to encounter a number of terms which can be a bit confusing at first. One term you will certainly encounter, and one which has already cropped up a few times in this chapter, is "font". If you look through a few publications, you will notice that the shape of any selected letter varies somewhat from one publication to another. In fact it is not just the letters that are different. There are marked differences in the figures, and even the punctuation marks. Each set of character shapes is a text font. With most d.t.p. programs you will have a number of fonts available as standard, probably with a great many more available as optional extras.

It is important to differentiate between text fonts and styles. Each font can have a number of different styles. As a few examples, text can be in bold (heavy) print, in light print, in italics, or underlined. These are just variations on a given font, and do not count as new fonts. Virtually all d.t.p. programs permit a range of fonts to be used, together with a wide range of text sizes. Even using just a couple of fonts, this permits a great deal of control to be exercised over the appearance of finished documents.

In Proportion

Two further terms you are likely to encounter are proportional spacing and kerning. These are similar, but definitely not different terms for the same thing. Proportional spacing is the more simple of the two. Obviously some letters take up more space than others. The letters "i" and "l" for example, are much thinner than the letters "W" and "M". With an ordinary typewriter or a computer printer used in its normal modes, this fact is ignored, and all letters are given the same amount of space. Thin characters appear well spaced out, and fat characters seem to be crammed together.

This is known as "monospacing", and d.t.p. programs do not normally work in this mode. Many d.t.p. programs do actually have the ability to use one or more monospaced fonts, but these are only used in a few special situations. They are sometimes required in technical and scientific publication work, and can be useful for tables and some types of list.

Desktop publishing programs normally operate on the basis of allocating each letter an amount of space which is in keeping with its width. This is proportional spacing, and it generally gives a much better appearance to the text.

Kerning takes proportional spacing a step further. Although you might think that the text would look as neat as possible with each letter given an amount of space which suits its width, in practice things are not quite this simple. Proportional spacing works well enough with letters that consist basically of vertical and horizontal lines, but it does not work so well with those that have sloping lines. In particular, there are problems when letters such as "A" and "W" are side-by-side. The gap between them tends to look too large.

In order to get the text to look absolutely right it is necessary to close up the gap slightly. The amount that the gap needs to be closed up is to some extent a subjective matter, and I suppose that text which looks perfect to one person might not look quite right to someone else. In general, the larger the text size, the more the text will need to be closed up on letter combinations of this type.

This closing up of the text is kerning. Most d.t.p. programs will automatically adjust the positions of letters so as to give a neater appearance to the text, and this is automatic kerning. As already pointed out, kerning is to some extent a subjective matter, and you might not always agree with the way in which the program kerns some of the text. There is often a facility that enables the positions of the text characters to be adjusted manually (manual kerning), so that the text can be "fine tuned" to what you subjectively judge to be perfection.

Going through pages of text adjusting the positions of hundreds of characters manually would be a very time consuming process, and manual kerning is not normally used in this way. It is mainly reserved for use where the program seems to have done things very badly, and for adjusting large text in headings and sub-headings. It is in small pieces of large sized text that any slight ineptitude in the kerning will be most apparent, and where careful manual kerning is most likely to be needed.

You will normally have the choice of justified or unjustified text. Unjustified text is straightforward lines of text with a ragged right hand margin, as obtained using an ordinary typewriter. With justified text additional spaces are placed between words so that all complete lines are the same length, and a neat right hand margin is produced. This book is an example of justified text. Most publications and documents are printed using justified text where this option is available, as it gives a neater and more professional appearance to the finished product. The main exception is where several narrow columns are used. Justified text can then result in large numbers of inserted spaces, and what are often rather scrappy looking results.

Sometimes the justification is controlled by having "switches" to control left and right hand justification. Left hand justification is then what would normally be considered unjustified text, while left and right justification gives justified text. Right hand justification only, gives a special effect where the right hand margin is neat and the left hand margin is ragged.

Normally where a long word is too long to fit into the space at the end of a line, it is placed on the subsequent line. If justification is used, this can result in a large number of spaces being added to pad out the line into which the word would not fit. This can give scrappy looking results. To avoid this, hyphenation is often used. This is where the word is split into two sections, with the first part at the end of one line, and the rest of the word on the subsequent line. A hyphen is used at the end of the first section of the word. Most publications that are printed with justified text are also hyphenated (including this one).

Desktop publishing programs mostly have an automatic hyphenation facility, but this may not always operate in a satisfactory way. Most automatic hyphenation systems are reasonably efficient, but few are guaranteed not to make even the occasional blunder. With the word "hyphenation" for instance, it might be hyphenated in the form "hyphe-nation", whereas most people would probably deem "hyphen-ation" or even "hyph-enation" to be better alternatives. Where the automatic hyphenation does not give the desired result, there should be no difficulty in doing some manual editing in order to sort things out.

Some rather quaint types of measurement are used in the printing industry, and when using a d.t.p. program you are almost certain to encounter one or two of these. The one you are most likely to come across is point size, which is mainly used as a means of selecting the required text size. Point sizes are in 1/72s of an inch, and simply dividing a point figure by 72 gives the height of capital letters in inches. Multiplying a point size by 0.353 gives the size in millimetres.

You may also encounter ems. An em is not a fixed size, and one em is equivalent to the point size of the font in use. It is mainly used when setting the spacing between the words, and by having it related to the font size it will automatically give lesser or greater spacing on smaller and larger character sizes (respectively). Ems are also used for other purposes, such as specifying the spacing between lines and paragraphs. Again, this has the advantage of giving greater spacing on larger text sizes, although you may be able to independently control the line and paragraph spacing at various points in a document should you wish to do so. Note that d.t.p. programs do not necessarily operate on the basis of simple single line spacing, double line spacing, etc. They mostly give much finer control than this. The gap between lines of text is known as the "leading" (pronounced "ledding") distance incidentally.

Chapter 2
D.T.P. HARDWARE

The usual advice to anyone setting up any form of computer system is to first find software that suits your requirements, and to then choose hardware (computer, monitor, printer, etc.) that will run the programs properly. This is sound advice in that by doing things the other way round you run the risk of buying a likely looking computer system only to find that there is no software for it that fully meets your needs. Presumably, if you buy software that meets your requirements, there will always be suitable hardware to run it. Software is not usually written for non-existent computers!

The only point to watch is that you do not buy bargain software for a computer that is obsolete. This might be a real bargain if you can also find some cheap "end of line" or secondhand hardware to run it on, but you could find yourself with a broken-down and unserviceable system before too long. Also bear in mind that with obsolete computer equipment there is little likelihood of an upgrade path to more modern equipment and software at some later stage. You may be forced to abandon your bargain system after a few years, complete with all its software and the files you have generated. In my opinion, for what it's worth, it is only worthwhile buying obsolete computer equipment if it is very cheap indeed.

Computers

Although the advice of choosing the software first and the hardware second is fine in theory, there is a practical difficulty in that few computer users can afford to simply go out and choose the ideal software and system for their requirements. When choosing the software you need to keep in mind the overall cost of the system, including the hardware, so that you stay within your budget. Compromises will probably have to be made somewhere, and possibly in every part of the system. This is especially the case for d.t.p. users, since d.t.p. software can cost however much you are prepared to pay. It is also demanding on the hardware, and it would be very easy to spend many thousands of pounds on the software or the hardware if you took a "money is no object" attitude.

In this chapter we will consider various types of computer equipment, and their suitability for d.t.p. applications. Obviously some people setting up a d.t.p. system already have computer equipment which they have been using for word processing, accounting, or whatever. For such people this chapter should still provide useful information about the suitability of their existing equipment for d.t.p. use, as well as providing helpful information for use when upgrading the system's hardware.

Practically any computer can be used for d.t.p. purposes, but some are much more suitable than others. Many of the early eight bit computers are not really suitable for this type of thing. Apart from other considerations, there is simply no good quality software of this type to run on them. Some of the better eight bit machines can handle d.t.p. quite well. There is some good quality d.t.p. software, etc., available for the Amstrad PCW and BBC 8 bit computers for example. On the other hand, sixteen bit computers are generally faster and more powerful than eight bit types, and in a "power" application such as d.t.p. a sixteen bit machine is likely to prove the better option.

If you are only interested in d.t.p. for producing fairly simple documents, and in the foreseeable future you will not need to do anything more than this, then a good eight bit system will probably handle things quite well. If you need a full-feature d.t.p. program that will run reasonably fast, or will need to progress to such a program in due course, then a sixteen bit computer is likely to be the better option. It is only fair to point out that the cost advantage of eight bit computers is nothing like as large as it once was. The cost of modern computer equipment tends to be governed more by items such as keyboards, cases, monitors, disk drives, etc., than it is by the particular microprocessor used (unless the computer happens to be fitted with an exceptionally powerful chip). One of the less expensive sixteen bit computers is therefore likely to prove a better buy. It may be slightly more expensive, but it should not become obsolete in the short to medium term, it should be faster in operation, and will probably have a better display (which is important in d.t.p. applications).

The choice of sixteen bit computers basically boils down to four ranges. Any of these are capable of running high quality d.t.p. programs. The Macintosh ("Mac") computers are widely regarded as being responsible for proving the viability of d.t.p., and for popularising this type of software. These computers are an excellent choice for the d.t.p. user, and are widely used for the production of books, magazines, and many other types of publication. Their main drawback is a relatively high cost. Some models with lower price tags have now been introduced, making them somewhat more affordable. They still seem to be somewhat more expensive than the other popular sixteen bit computers though. They are certainly an excellent choice for d.t.p. applications if you can afford them.

Although at one time the Amiga computers had a relatively small software base, there now seems to be plenty of programs to run on them, including some good d.t.p. types. The same is also true of the Atari ST range. These both provide a good low cost entry into sixteen bit computing and high quality d.t.p. Some peripherals (external disk drives and hard disk drives in particular) have tended to be quite expensive for these machines in the past. This meant that buying a basic system was quite cheap, but the cost soon mounted if you made a few additions to the setup. The introduction of some "third party" add-ons for these computers has tended to force prices down, making them a more attractive proposition for someone who requires something more than a pretty basic system. They are perhaps less expandable and ultimately less capable than some other sixteen bit computers, but they are well able to handle most applications, including d.t.p.

Last, and by no means least, there are the IBM PCs and the numerous "compatibles" on the market. Although PC (personal computer) is a term that can be used to describe any fairly powerful microcomputer, the IBM PCs and compatibles are now popularly known as "PCs". These computers have tended to be rather maligned in the past, mainly because the specifications of the original IBM PCs were not particularly impressive. They are based on the 8088 microprocessor, which is the least powerful in that particular series of devices. This gave little more computing power than the better eight bit machines could provide. The screen display was also rather limited, being a simple text only type.

It would be a mistake to judge modern PCs by the specifications of the early models. Modern PCs have microprocessors that run two or more times faster than the originals. Also, many are now based on more powerful versions of the 8088 microprocessor, giving a further boost in speed. Generally speaking, the more powerful the microprocessor used, the greater the cost of a PC. It has to be remembered though, that these computers are manufactured by a substantial number of companies. This gives a tremendous variation in cost for any given type of PC. In order of power and price (starting with the least powerful) the microprocessors are the 8088, 8086, 80286, 80386SX, 80386, and 80486.

As d.t.p. tends to be very demanding on the microprocessor, there is a definite advantage in having one of the more powerful PCs when running this type of software. On the other hand, the most powerful PCs are very expensive. The simpler (XT type) PCs which are based on the 8088 and 8086 are capable of running most d.t.p. programs for the PCs, but may be a little sluggish at carrying out some operations. My preference would be for an AT type PC based on a reasonably fast (about 12MHz or more) 80286 microprocessor. I have used several powerful d.t.p. programs on a computer of this type, and it has coped very well. If funds run to the purchase of a 80386SX, 80386, or an 80486 based computer, then these should run that much faster and better.

The PCs have established themselves as the standard business computers, and one reason for this is probably the ease with which they can be expanded. In particular, it is usually quite straightforward to add an extra floppy disk drive or a hard disk drive, and with most models these can be fitted internally. Although the original display was a monochrome text only type, these days there are many display options, including several that are well suited to d.t.p. applications (displays are discussed in more detail later).

It is difficult to compare PCs with the other sixteen bit computers in terms of price, as PCs cover such a wide price range. At the time of writing, the cheapest PCs complete with a monochrome monitor cost only about three hundred pounds, while the most expensive systems are around twenty times this figure. Assuming you do not opt for a particularly advanced model or one of the more expensive makes, a PC system has a cost that is broadly comparable to Atari ST and Commodore Amiga systems.

Displays

There tends to be a lot of terminology associated with most aspects of computing, and displays are no exception. Most of the terminology associated with displays is either pretty straightforward, or is not something you really need to know about in any detail. By displays we simply mean the monitor and the circuitry in the computer that drives it. In the case of a home computer, the monitor might actually be a television set driven via a modulator (the latter often being an internal part of the computer). For d.t.p. applications a good quality display is a real asset. Television sets mostly have quite large screen sizes, but do not have the resolution and general quality to match. In general, the better quality television receivers do not provide a level of quality that equals that of an inexpensive monitor. Most can not even display eighty column text clearly. For any serious computing work a proper monitor is definitely preferable to a television set plus a modulator.

"Graphics" is a term you will often encounter, and it is merely the ability of a display to produce drawings of some kind, rather than being limited to text characters. The vast majority of displays can produce graphics (the main exception being the original PC type), but their capabilities in this respect vary enormously. Some are simple monochrome displays of the true black and white type (although many monitors actually produce amber or green displays rather than white types). Other displays can produce a few colours when utilized with suitable colour monitors, while at the top end of the market there are types which can produce over two hundred colours from a choice of around a quarter of a million or more colours.

It would seem to be a reasonable assumption that a text only display will suffice if the documents to be produced do not contain any drawings or diagrams. In reality this is not the case. This is something that depends on the d.t.p. program, and there has been software of this type that can operate with a text only display. However, most d.t.p. programs try to give an accurate WYSIWYG (what you see is what you get, pronounced "wessywig") display. This generally makes it easier to lay out pages, and enables the final result to be properly assessed before it is printed out. Repeatedly printing out pages, checking them, making minor alterations, and then reprinting takes a lot of time and can be quite costly.

In order to produce a WYSIWYG display, even a text only type, it is necessary to have some graphics capability. Remember that most text only displays give a single font in a single size. At best there will only be a few sizes of lettering and small range of different fonts available. Most d.t.p. programs can handle dozens of different fonts in dozens or even hundreds of sizes. In order to give a reasonably accurate representation of all these fonts in different sizes on the screen, the letters must be generated as simple graphics objects. This obviously requires a display with graphics capability.

While a good WYSIWYG display has clear advantages, it does have a drawback. This is simply that changes to a layout can require a lot of recalculating in order to produce the modified page on the screen.

This makes WYSIWYG systems very much slower in operation than those which provide simple text displays. Provided the d.t.p. program is run on a reasonably powerful computer, a WYSIWYG display should not slow things down to an unacceptable degree. Most users happily trade off some loss of speed for the added convenience of a WYSIWYG screen.

Resolution

An important factor in deciding the quality and usefulness of a display is its resolution. Both text and graphics displays are made up from thousands of dots. If you look carefully at a computer display you will probably be able to see the individual dots, or "pixels" as they are termed. Having a large number of small dots enables graphics displays to produce quite high quality images. It is only fair to point out that high resolution graphics displays are high resolution only in relation to other graphics displays. Compared with good quality printers and plotters, or hand produced artwork come to that, they are still rather crude. The low and medium resolution displays are really very crude, with diagonal lines that have very pronounced stepping, and curves that are far from smooth. Trying to display a full d.t.p. page on one of these usually gives what is just a jumbled mess that is very hard to interpret. True high resolution displays can just about produce a full page of readable text, provided the text size is not exceptionally small, or the page size unusually large.

Graphics resolution is specified as so many horizontal pixels by so many lines of pixels (e.g. 640 × 480 means 480 lines of 640 pixels). The resolution of text displays, incidentally, is normally just given in the form of the number of characters per line by the number of lines of characters (e.g. a text resolution of 80 × 25 means 25 lines of text with up to 80 characters per line). Two text displays having the same number of characters per line and lines of characters might not have the same number of pixels making up the screen. One might have a higher resolution than the other, with more pixels per character. Hence higher resolution displays often give superior text quality, even though in specification sheets they might both simply be given as 80 × 25 displays (or whatever).

When dealing with monitors you will often encounter various frequencies quoted. These are the number of lines produced per second, the number of complete screens-full per second, etc. You do not normally need to bother too much about this sort of thing. You normally buy a monitor for a computer simply on the basis of it being compatible with a certain model, or certain display standards in the case of the PCs.

When studying the specifications of colour monitors you may encounter references to their "dot pitch". In theory, the smaller the dot pitch, the better the display quality will be, especially when displaying high resolution images. In practice the dot pitch is not all-important, and other factors affect the display quality. The only way in which the quality of a monitor can be properly judged is to try it out in practice and subjectively assess it. Specifications such as the dot pitch are not reliable indicators of display quality.

Colour or Monochrome

For d.t.p. purposes good screen resolution is a definite bonus, and if possible it is well worth paying the extra money to get the best resolution that the computer in question can offer. Colour is probably of lesser importance. If you are only producing monochrome documents, which is probably all that most d.t.p. users produce, then colour is likely to be of little benefit at all. Colour is sometimes used as a method of showing (say) a block of text that has been selected in order to edit it in some way, by showing the relevant text in a different screen colour. Monochrome systems generally manage this type of thing quite well though, using techniques such as inverse video (i.e. dark letters on a light background instead of the usual light lettering on a dark background), or underlining the "blocked" text.

If you are going to produce colour documents, then a colour screen could be a much greater asset. Colour is still not essential, and countless full colour documents have been produced on monochrome computer systems. You indicate the colours required for various pieces of text, diagrams, or whatever, and they are printed out in these colours. You can obviously not preview the colours correctly on the screen though, and a colour print-out must be made in order to check that everything is as it should be.

The screen types available is something that varies from computer to computer. On eight bit computers the maximum colour resolution is usually something in the region of 320 pixels by 256 pixels in up to four colours. Remember that the quoted number of colours always includes the background colour, so four colours is the background colour plus up to three foreground colours. This sort of resolution is far from ideal for d.t.p. purposes. Usually there is a monochrome option which offers higher resolution (typically about 640 by 256 pixels), and this is probably the better choice for d.t.p. use. In fact d.t.p. programs for eight bit computers will often only operate in the monochrome screen mode. The Amstrad PCW range are unusual in that they only offer a single monochrome screen mode. This is of relatively high resolution though, and is well suited to d.t.p. use.

Sixteen bit computers almost invariably offer a range of modes from low/medium resolution colour through to high resolution colour and monochrome modes. In some cases there may be no monochrome modes as such, but if a monochrome monitor is what you use, a monochrome display is all you get (albeit with various shades of grey in some cases). Provided the software supports a monochrome display, then this should be good enough. The Atari ST computers are slightly unusual in that they support 320 × 200 and 640 × 200 pixel multi-colour modes, or a totally separate 640 × 400 monochrome mode using a special monitor. Many d.t.p. programs will run in either the higher resolution colour mode or the monochrome mode, and the latter is probably the more popular choice for d.t.p. use. The Atari ST monochrome display is widely regarded as one of the best displays currently available on a low cost computer, and it would seem to fully justify this reputation. Given the choice of a colour display, or a much higher resolution monochrome display, I think that I would always be drawn towards the monochrome type for d.t.p. use.

PC Display Standards

The PCs and compatibles are now widely used for d.t.p. work, and are probably the most popular computers for this application (or just about any other application for that matter). These computers can be a bit confusing with regard to their displays, as there are several types of display card available for them. These include several standard display boards, and a number of specials which offer very high resolutions but do not conform to the IBM standards. Some of these special display adaptors are high resolution (mainly monochrome) types primarily designed for d.t.p. use. These are obviously ideal for d.t.p. work provided your d.t.p. program actually supports the particular high resolution display board you wish to use. Most of these boards are actually supplied with driver software that enables them to be used with popular d.t.p. and graphics programs. If the program does not support the display board, the display board may have support for the program.

Most users find that one of the ordinary display boards satisfies their requirements. If you require a very high resolution display, especially a multi-colour type, you will probably need to pay out a great deal of money. In fact a display board of this type plus a matching monitor can easily cost substantially more than the rest of the hardware in the system. Exactly what is available in the way of high resolution display cards, and the programs that are compatible with them, seems to be constantly changing. It is a matter of consulting the computer press and local dealers in order to find out just what is available at the time you wish to purchase a display system. Do not overlook the alternative of an enhanced VGA board. As we shall see shortly, these offer a very cost effective solution to high resolution multi-colour graphics.

The original PCs had a monochrome text only display, known as the MDA (monochrome display adaptor) card. This is now obsolete, and is unlikely to be of any use with d.t.p. programs. There were two types of display which ousted the MDA type. One of these was the IBM CGA (colour graphics adaptor), while the other was the Hercules type, produced by the company of the same name. The CGA board has two graphics modes. One of these is a multi-colour mode, but it only offers four colours (including the background colour). The resolution is 320 × 200 pixels, which makes it considerably less than ideal for d.t.p. applications. The other graphics mode is a monochrome one offering a slightly improved resolution of 640 × 200 pixels. This is better suited to d.t.p. programs, and although its resolution is far lower than would be ideal, it has been used successfully by many d.t.p. users. The Hercules display is a monochrome type which offers a graphics resolution of 720 × 348 pixels. This display is quite well suited to d.t.p. use, and represents a very inexpensive means of obtaining fairly high resolution.

The shortcomings of the CGA standard led to the development of the EGA (enhanced graphics adaptor) card. This offers the same modes as the CGA type, plus some higher resolution types. In particular there is a 640 × 350 pixel monochrome type, and a sixteen colour mode offering the same resolution. EGA boards offer quite good results in d.t.p. and general graphics applications, but this standard has now been somewhat overshadowed by the more recent VGA (versatile graphics array) display adaptor.

These days a VGA display is the obvious choice for many applications, including d.t.p. For d.t.p. use the screen mode that is of most interest is the 640 × 480 pixel sixteen colour mode. This gives somewhat better resolution than an EGA display, and VGA types also tend to be somewhat swifter in operation. A VGA card and colour monitor can now be obtained at quite reasonable cost. For d.t.p. applications many users opt for a monochrome monitor. This gives quite a low cost display having good resolution, and capable of displaying grey scales instead of colours. Incidentally, VGA cards can provide all the earlier IBM screen modes (MDA, CGA, and EGA), plus a Hercules emulation in most cases.

Virtually all VGA cards now support extensions of the VGA standard, known by such names "enhanced" and "super" VGA. These offer higher resolutions or more colours, or both in some cases. The most common enhanced VGA mode is one offering 800 × 600 pixels with a maximum of 16 colours on screen at once. Many boards also offer a higher resolution mode with fewer colours. The resolution is normally 1024 × 768 pixels with up to 16 colours (fewer colours than this on some boards). This sort of resolution is suitable for demanding d.t.p. and CAD applications, but in order to avoid eye strain and fully utilize such high resolution a fairly sizeable monitor is needed.

The drawback of the enhanced modes is that they seem to be something less than fully standardised. When running a setup or installation program, selecting the 800 × 600 16-colour mode for one enhanced VGA board does not seem to guarantee results with a different enhanced VGA board that supports this mode. Looking on the bright side, enhanced VGA boards are normally supplied with some disks that contain useful utilities plus drivers for popular software (typically GEM, Windows, Ventura, AutoCAD, WordPerfect and Lotus 1-2-3). Also, many graphics programs now support the more popular of these cards, and support for them seems to be increasing. Their popularity is such that this trend seems likely to continue, or even to accelerate. Provided you obtain one of the more common enhanced VGA cards, or perhaps one that is based on the same chip set as a popular type, you are likely to find that it is well supported. As always though, it is advisable to get the software that suits your requirements, and to then purchase the hardware needed to make it function in the desired manner.

Pan and Zoom

Although a very high resolution screen is a major asset for d.t.p. work, it is possible to get by with relatively low resolutions. Although most d.t.p.

programs for the PCs seem to recommend the use of a VGA screen for instance, most are actually usable with a CGA display in its 640 x 200 pixel monochrome mode. This sort of resolution is not really adequate for displaying full pages of text, complete with readable text in the right font. The standard way around this problem is to have a rather crude representation of full pages, with the text represented by short lines, with no attempt to produce readable letters. This is of no value for checking that everything is letter perfect, but it does give a good overall impression of the final printed page.

In order to check pages in detail there is normally a pan and zoom feature. The zoom facility permits part of a page to be viewed in great detail so that the text can be checked for typographical errors, and to ensure that the right fonts, letter styles, and text sizes have been selected. With some graphics programs you can select any zoom ratio, but with d.t.p. programs there is normally a choice of three or four preset zoom ratios. This is usually quite adequate in practice, and permits the program to run faster than would be possible with user selected zoom ratios. The pan facility enables the part of the page that is viewed to be altered.

Even small shifts in the viewed area tend to take a great deal of recalculating in order to produce the new screen display. Consequently, unless the d.t.p. program is very well written and the computer used is a very powerful one, panning and zooming are likely to be something less than instant. With some d.t.p. systems they are very slow indeed. Panning and zooming are therefore something less than total substitutes for a high resolution display using a high quality monitor. On the other hand, even with most high resolution displays it is not possible to properly represent a full page on the screen. Also, even if this is possible, detailed editing can be decidedly fiddly with a full page display. Therefore, even with the highest resolution displays, a certain amount of panning and zooming is still likely to be necessary. A good display enables it to be kept to a minimum though.

Input Devices

Many types of computing are spent entering data via the keyboard. Although with d.t.p. programs you might expect to spend much of the time typing text into the program, it is not usually done like this. It is possible to type text direct into d.t.p. programs, but in general the text is produced using a text editor or a word processor (as explained more fully in Chapter 1). The text is stored on disk, and the disk files are loaded into the d.t.p. program. The ability to add and edit text using the d.t.p. program is included mainly to permit minor corrections and alterations to be made, rather than as the main means of entering text. Of course, you may still spend a lot of time at the keyboard entering the text for documents, and a good keyboard is then a decided asset. On the other hand, you might be making up documents based on text files supplied by other people, and the keyboard may then be needed relatively little.

All the d.t.p. programs I have encountered permit full control of the program via the keyboard. In many cases though, this is a rather slow and cumbersome way of handling things. A mouse represents a much more convenient way of controlling the cursor (which is an on-screen pointer). For those who are unfamiliar with these devices it should perhaps be explained that a mouse is basically just a small box which is moved around on the desktop, with the on-screen cursor following the movements of the mouse. This might not seem to be much better than using the cursor keys, but in practice a mouse enables the cursor to be rapidly moved from any part of the screen to any other part of the screen. Once the cursor has been positioned in roughly the right area of the screen, there is no difficulty in making fine adjustments to precisely position it.

Some mice are actually supported by software drivers that make rapid cursor movement and fine control of its position even easier. These have a so-called "ballistic" effect, which simply means that rapid movements of the mouse cause the cursor to move a relatively large distance. Slow movements of the mouse result in relatively small displacements of the cursor. When moving the cursor from one part of the screen to another you naturally tend to move the mouse quite fast, and with the ballistic effect only a small mouse movement is needed in order to move the cursor even from one corner of the screen to the opposite corner. On the other hand, when making fine adjustments there is a natural tendency to move the mouse very slowly and carefully. This makes relatively large mouse movements necessary in order to produce quite small shifts in the cursor's position. This makes accurate positioning of the cursor very easy.

In other words, the ballistic effect enables the cursor to be shifted very quickly from one area of the screen to another, but it does so without making fine adjustments of the cursor's position very tricky. The software often permits the degree to which the ballistic effect is applied to be varied, and removed altogether if desired. It is certainly a useful feature to have available, but it does not suit all users.

Mice are usually fitted with one, two, or three switches of the push button type (like outsize computer keyboard keys). The function of the mouse buttons depends on the application in use. Typically you would use the mouse to point to the desired option on an on-screen "menu" (which is simply a list of options displayed on the screen), and then press one of the buttons to confirm selection of that option. There are many ways in which the mouse buttons can be used though, and it is necessary to consult the manuals for your software in order to determine exactly how the mouse is used with your programs.

Sixteen-bit computers are often supplied complete with a mouse. The main exceptions are the PCs and compatibles which are sometimes supplied with a mouse as part of the standard system, but it is more normally an optional extra. In some cases the mouse has to be obtained separately from a third party supplier. It is unusual for eight bit computers to be supplied complete with a mouse, but there is at least one mouse available for most of the more popular eight-bit computers. However, do not assume that d.t.p. software will have support for one of these third party mice. Check this point carefully before actually buying one. Mice are by no means the most expensive pieces of computer equipment, and if a d.t.p. program has support for a mouse, it will probably be well worthwhile making any additional expenditure needed in order to add a suitable mouse to the system.

Digitisers

Digitising tablets are absolute pointing devices, rather than relative types (like mice). In other words, whereas a mouse can only be used to indicate movement in a certain direction, a digitising tablet deals in definite screen positions. If you lift a mouse from its mat, move it to a new position, and then replace it on the mat, the on-screen pointer will not move. With a digitising tablet, if you raise the "pen" or puck from the tablet, and then move it, the on-screen pointer will not move. However, as soon as you lower the "pen" or puck down onto the tablet the pointer will immediately jump to the appropriate position on the screen.

Most software is no easier to use with a digitising tablet than it is with a mouse, and they then offer no real advantages over mice. As digitisers are about ten times more expensive than mice, this has led to them being far less popular. Where a program does properly support a digitising tablet, it might be well worthwhile paying the extra money for one. A tablet is very useful for use with illustration programs, etc., where it is sometimes necessary to trace existing artwork into the computer. The ability of a tablet to operate using a "pen", or "stylus" as it is more correctly termed, makes it more suitable for applications where free-hand drawing is involved. Most people, even after gaining much experience with a mouse, find it difficult to use for free-hand drawing. A stylus is much better for this type of thing, being very much like using an ordinary pen or pencil.

For d.t.p. applications many people find a digitising tablet and a stylus much easier to use than a mouse. With many d.t.p. programs a good deal of the time is spent indicating frames into which text or graphics must be imported, indicating blocks of text that must be moved or altered in some way, and this general type of thing. A stylus probably represents the quickest and easiest tool for this type of thing. There is no need to use a large graphics tablet for most d.t.p. applications, and one of the smallest units should be perfectly adequate. Bear in mind though, that if you will also be using the graphics tablet with an illustration program or some other form of drawing software, this might require a large graphics tablet.

Tracker Balls

Tracker balls are a relatively rare form of pointing device. A unit of this type is, more or less, an upside-down mouse of the type which has a weighted ball to detect the movement of the device. In other words, the ball is on the top side of the unit, and is usually operated with the thumb or palm of the hand. The buttons are, of course, also on the top side of the unit so that they can be easily reached by the operator. The advantage of this system is that it occupies relatively little of the desktop, since the unit remains stationary. Even given that a tracker ball is usually much larger than any mouse, it still requires much less space.

Although tracker balls are potentially very good pointing devices, there can be a few slight snags in practice. One is simply that with your hand moving around but the buttons in fixed positions, the buttons are not always where they can be easily reached with your fingers. The units that have balls which are intended for operation by the user's thumb overcome this problem, but many users seem to find accurate positioning of the cursor difficult with these units. A tracker ball might be well suited to you and your software, but it would be a good idea to try one out and satisfy yourself of its suitability before parting with any money.

Printers

In order to undertake d.t.p. work you do not necessarily require a printer. You can simply use a suitable d.t.p. program to make up disk files of all the pages, and then have these printed by an agency. The printing can be done on anything from a relatively inexpensive laser printer to very high quality (and costly) printing machines offering extremely high quality results. Probably most d.t.p. users do not do things this way, and print out documents on their own printers. This obviously depends on such factors as the print quality required, and on the number of copies needed. Cost is also a major factor, and while professionally printed documents of very high print quality are something we would all like to produce, for many d.t.p. users the cost of this kind of thing is still far too high for serious contemplation. Even if you should opt for printing via an agency, your own printer can still be a decided asset. It enables page proofs to be produced and checked at low cost, before committing yourself to costly printing processes.

These days most types of printer are suitable for use with d.t.p. programs. There is always a possibility of incompatibility between a particular d.t.p. program and a specific printer, and this is something that should be checked before buying software and equipment. The only common kind of printer which is totally unsuitable for d.t.p. work is the daisywheel type. These have to be regarded as text only printers. Some models do in fact have some graphics capability, but they are generally too slow when used in this way to be of any practical value for graphics work. Remember that even if a document is a text only type, the d.t.p. program will almost certainly drive the printer in its graphics mode. In the same way that multiple text fonts and sizes can only be produced on most displays using the graphics mode, and effectively having each letter as a graphics object, most printers can only handle things in basically the same way.

The cheapest printers that will produce hard copy from d.t.p. programs are nine pin dot-matrix printers. This name is perhaps a little misleading in that several types of printer produce the pages from a matrix of dots. This is essentially the same approach that is used with screen displays and their pixels. However, in the case of printers the term "dot" seems to be used instead of pixel.

A nine pin dot-matrix printer has a print head with a vertical row of nine retractable pins that are controlled by a built-in microprocessor. The print head strikes a ribbon in front of the paper, and in this respect it is a simple impact printing system much like an ordinary typewriter. There is a big difference though, in that a dot matrix printer can not print complete characters in one go. Typically the characters are made up from a nine high by five across matrix of dots, and the printhead therefore has to be hammered against the ribbon and paper five times in order to produce each character. Each time the printhead is activated, only the appropriate pins must be advanced, so that the required pattern of dots is built up.

This could give the impression that dot-matrix printers are very slow, but they can actually print at respectably fast speeds. They are by no means the fastest of printers, but it is generally only much more expensive printers that produce printouts at a vastly greater rate. The main problem with nine pin dot-matrix printers is that their basic print quality is not very good. The dots are quite large by printer standards, and there are gaps between them. Looking at a page of print from one of these devices it is not usually difficult to see the individual dots, and the way each character is produced from a matrix of dots.

All current nine pin machines seem to offer higher quality print modes, or NLQ (near letter quality) modes as they are generally termed. These operate using a double strike process, where each dot is produced by having the printhead first strike normally, and then strike again slightly offset from the original position. In fact this process can be extended, with the printhead striking three or four times in order to produce each dot, with a different offset distance and (or) direction being used for each strike. If this multi-strike method is applied in a sensible fashion it can produce a surprising increase in the print quality. The gaps between the dots are filled in, and close inspection of the characters is needed before the individual dots become apparent.

Obviously there is a limit to the increase in quality that this method can produce, and although the quality is acceptable for many purposes, it is still inadequate for applications that require very high quality printing. Another point to keep in mind is that this multiple strike method inevitably slows down the printing process. With two to four times as many strikes being required, the printing speed is (more or less) reduced by a factor of two to four times. A printer that can operate at a respectably fast rate in its normal ("draft") mode will be far less impressive in its highest quality mode.

Most d.t.p. programs do not drive printers in their text modes, and the text modes of a dot-matrix printer might seem to be irrelevant. However, the dot-matrix approach can be applied to graphics as well as it can be applied to printing standard text characters. Also, the multi-strike methods can be applied to graphics in order to give improved print quality at the expense of reduced printing speed. Most d.t.p. programs will therefore operate quite happily with nine pin dot-matrix printers, and will produce text of any font, style, and size within the repertoire of the program. Graphics can also be included where necessary.

The maximum resolution from a nine pin printer is at best 240 × 216 dots to the inch. This is not that much less than the resolution of some expensive laser printers, but these figures rather flatter the capabilities of nine pin printers. It has to be remembered that the dot size is relatively large, and this factor is just as important as the number of dots per inch. The subjective print quality is therefore nothing like as good as the printers that operate at the slightly higher resolution of 300 dots per inch by 300 dots per inch. You should also bear in mind that not all nine pin printers have a maximum resolution as high as 240 dots per inch by 216 dots per inch. Even if the printer can manage this resolution, the d.t.p. program might not operate it in that mode.

There is a potential problem when using a nine pin dot-matrix printer in that it might not be compatible with the d.t.p. program. Problems with incompatibility are less likely to arise if you use one of the popular makes and models of printer. Alternatively, many printers offer compatibility with a popular make and model of printer. Provided the emulation is an accurate one, a printer of this type should be usable with virtually all d.t.p. programs. Most nine pin printers now seem to be graphics compatible with the popular Epson range of printers, and Epson compatible printers should be usable with virtually any d.t.p. program.

Figure 2.1 shows a sample printout made with a nine pin dot-matrix printer using a high resolution mode.

24 Pins

One step up in quality from the nine pin dot-matrix printers come the twenty-four pin variety. These have two vertical rows of pins that are staggered slightly. The increase in quality is not quite as great as the difference between nine and twenty-four pins would suggest. In effect, there are three extra pins in the row to give increased print quality, and two rows of pins in order to double the print speed. Twenty-four pin printers therefore give somewhat better print quality than the nine pin types, and are faster in operation. This is only a generalisation though, and the fastest of nine pin printers can easily out-pace the slower twenty-four pin types. Also, the subjective print quality of a really good nine pin machine might be better than that of a cheap twenty-four pin type.

The maximum resolution of most twenty-four pin printers is 360 × 180 dots to the inch. Some can operate at 360 × 360 dots to the inch, which is better than most laser printers. Like the resolution figures for nine pin printers, these rather flatter the true capabilities of twenty-four pin printers. In common with nine pin machines, the dot size is rather large when compared to the maximum resolutions in terms of dots per inch. This means that these printers are not quite as precise as their resolution figures would suggest. Subjectively assessed, the print quality is not normally anything like as good as 300 d.p.i. printers which use other methods of producing the image.

The software writers seemed to be rather slow in responding to the popularity of twenty-four pin

CHAPTER 5

PC REPAIRS

There is an old joke about the woman who was amazed that her old broom had lasted thirty years - and it only needed two new handles and seven new heads! I suppose that the modular construction of PCs leaves them open to the same sort of claim. Over the years you can put in a new display card here, a replacement disk drive there, and maybe even a new motherboard in the fullness of time. Five or six years later the computer will still be going strong, and will probably have a specification well above that of the original machine, but the case might be the only survivor from the original hardware!

The PC's modular method of construction aids the DIY repairer. Even if you can not mend the particular item that is faulty, then it can instead be completely replaced. This might seem to be a wasteful approach, and to an extent I suppose that it is. Being realistic about modern electronics in general, current production processes are so efficient that many pieces of equipment can now be produced at very low cost. Repairing equipment can take a lot of man hours from highly skilled (and well paid) service engineers, making it a costly process. Modern production processes are designed to make the manufacture of equipment as cheap as possible, with servicing usually being of only secondary importance. This makes fitting replacement parts on some circuit boards quite difficult.

Obviously each case has to be assessed on its own merits. Throwing away a high capacity hard disk drive that has become faulty just outside the guarantee period and replacing it will a new one would not be a cost effective way of handling the problem. At the other extreme, something like a parallel printer port card that has become faulty after several years use is probably not worth repairing. It would only cost a few pounds to replace it with a new one.

There is a big incentive to undertake DIY repairs. The cost of professional repairs on PCs can be quite high, with the minimum fee sometimes being higher than the cost of any one of an average PCs component parts. Carriage costs to and from the service centre can be high, as can calling in an engineer to provide on-site maintenance. While I would not advocate prodding around inside expensive

Fig. 2.1 120 × 144 d.p.i. output from a nine pin printer. The smallest text sizes are barely readable, and the larger sizes are a bit rough at the edges (literally)

printers, and it is only relatively recently that there has been widespread support for them in graphics programs. Even so, not all programs are capable of operating these printers at their maximum resolution. Many twenty-four pin types offer a degree of compatibility with nine pin printers, but in my experience feeding nine pin output to a twenty-four pin printer gives very poor results. The aspect ratio becomes severely distorted, and the printing is something less than solid. Without a proper twenty-four pin driver, a d.t.p. program is unlikely to produce usable results with one of these printers.

A possible reason for dot-matrix printers (regardless of their number of pins) not producing results quite as good as one might expect, is that they use what is really a rather crude form of impact printing. This gives dots that are less well defined than they might be. The state of the ribbon has a considerable effect on the print quality. A new ribbon gives good black printing, but can tend to over-ink, possibly with pronounced smudging in places. Results are generally best with a ribbon that is slightly used, so that good black printing is produced, but without any over-inking and general smudging. With an old ribbon the printing will be decidely pale, and the individual dots may well be rather more apparent than they should be. There may even be odd pieces of the printing missing here and there.

It is possible to obtain carbon ribbons for some dot-matrix printers. These are based on thin plastic instead of the usual fabric ribbon, and actually look more like recording tape than a printer ribbon. The coating is a thin film of ink though, much like that on carbon paper. These are usually very long, but are designed to go through the printer once and then be thrown away. Fabric ribbons normally go backwards and forwards through the printer repeatedly, with the inking getting steadily weaker. This once-only operation gives consistent print quality, and the thinness of the backing material helps to give sharply defined dots. The quality obtained with these ribbons is therefore better and more consistent than that obtained using fabric ribbons. Running costs are generally somewhat higher though, and this type of ribbon is not available for all dot-matrix machines.

Figure 2.2 shows a sample printout produced using a twenty-four pin dot-matrix printer driven in its highest resolution mode. This is significantly better than the output from most nine pin machines, particularly on the smaller text sizes.

CHAPTER 5

PC REPAIRS

There is an old joke about the woman who was amazed that her old broom had lasted thirty years - and it only needed two new handles and seven new heads! I suppose that the modular construction of PCs leaves them open to the same sort of claim. Over the years you can put in a new display card here, a replacement disk drive there, and maybe even a new motherboard in the fullness of time. Five or six years later the computer will still be going strong, and will probably have a specification well above that of the original machine, but the case might be the only survivor from the original hardware!

The PC's modular method of construction aids the DIY repairer. Even if you can not mend the particular item that is faulty, then it can instead be completely replaced. This might seem to be a wasteful approach, and to an extent I suppose that it is. Being realistic about modern electronics in general, current production processes are so efficient that many pieces of equipment can now be produced at very low cost. Repairing equipment can take a lot of man hours from highly skilled (and well paid) service engineers, making it a costly process. Modern production processes are designed to make the manufacture of equipment as cheap as possible, with servicing usually being of only secondary importance. This makes fitting replacement parts on some circuit boards quite difficult.

Obviously each case has to be assessed on its own merits. Throwing away a high capacity hard disk drive that has become faulty just outside the guarantee period and replacing it will a new one would not be a cost effective way of handling the problem. At the other extreme, something like a parallel printer port card that has become faulty after several years use is probably not worth repairing. It would only cost a few pounds to replace it with a new one.

There is a big incentive to undertake DIY repairs. The cost of professional repairs on PCs can be quite high, with the minimum fee sometimes being higher than the cost of any one of an average PCs component parts. Carriage costs to and from the service centre can be high, as can calling in an engineer to provide on-site maintenance. While I would not advocate prodding around inside expensive computer equipment if you are not rea-

Fig. 2.2 180 d.p.i. output from a 24 pin dot-matrix printer. The smallest print sizes are just about readable, but not very neat

Ink-Jets

The way in which ink-jet printers operate is very simple in principle, but it is quite difficult to produce practical products using this system. Some of the early ink-jet printers were not very good in some respects. The problems mainly centred around clogging of the ink-jet nozzles which often resulted in very poor quality printing, and generally inconsistent results. This has resulted in ink-jet printers getting a rather poor reputation which is not really deserved by the current printers which use this method.

The printhead of an ink-jet printer consists basically of an ink reservoir plus a number of minute nozzles. These are equivalent to the pins in the printhead of a dot-matrix printer. The number of nozzles can be roughly equivalent to nine or twenty-four pin printers, but it is often much higher. The Hewlett Packard Deskjet+ printer that I often use, for example, has fifty nozzles giving 300 × 300 dots to the inch resolution. Some ink-jet printers have even higher resolution than this. As the printhead is moved across the paper, the appropriate nozzles are activated at each point, building up the required image in standard pixel fashion. The jets of ink are normally produced using electrical heating elements which boil the ink, causing it to squirt out of the nozzles.

This method of printing has its advantages and disadvantages. On the plus side, it gives high quality printing. The dots can be made fine enough to justify the resolutions of the higher quality machines, and the non-impact method of printing gives well defined dots. The blackness of the print is consistent right up to the point where the ink reservoir becomes exhausted. Good quality ink-jet printers will often produce a print quality that is high enough for the final document, or to produce pages that can be used in a mass printing process. It is only where very high quality results are needed that some other means will have to be used for the final product.

Ink-jet printers are reasonably small and light. They will certainly fit onto most computer desktops without any difficulty. Their non-impact printing system is very quiet. In fact the actual printing part of these machines is virtually silent, and the noise

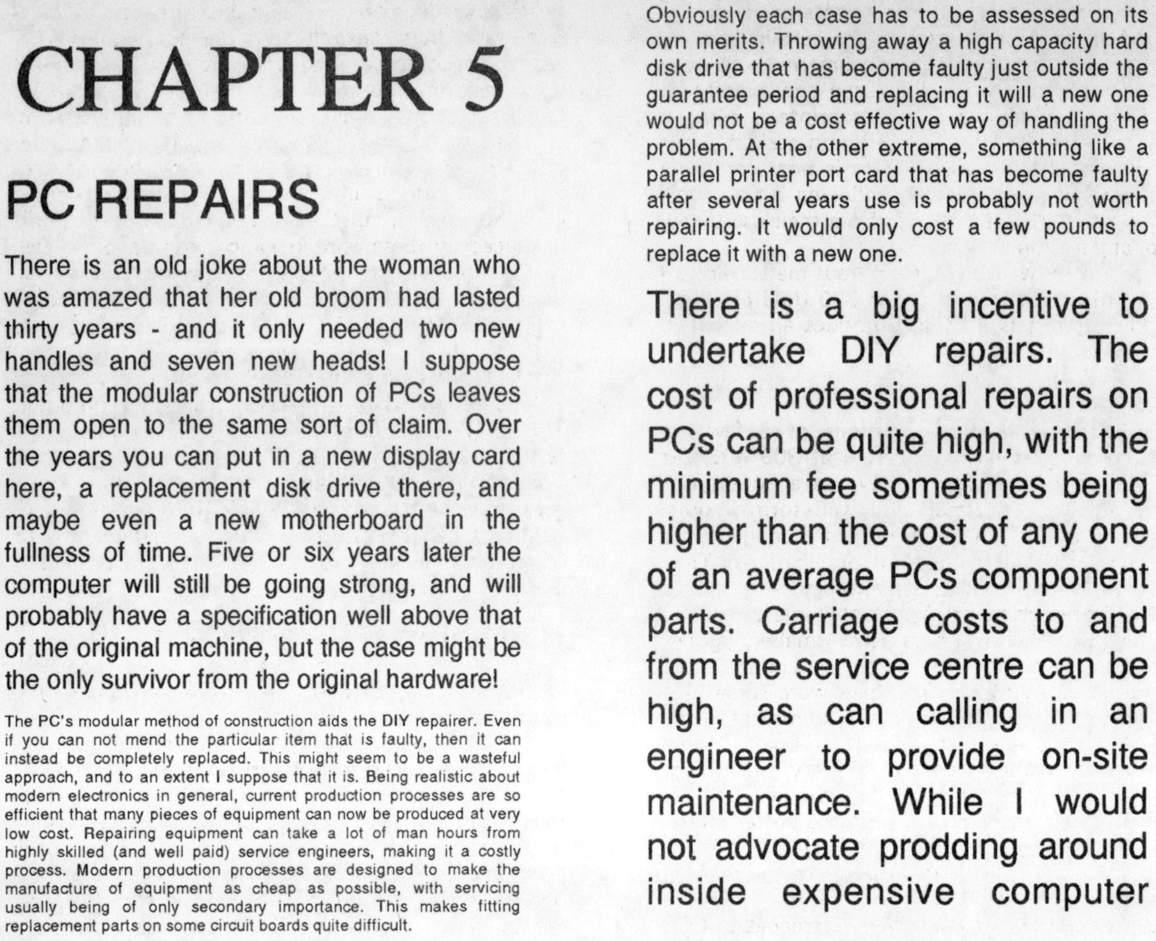

CHAPTER 5

PC REPAIRS

There is an old joke about the woman who was amazed that her old broom had lasted thirty years - and it only needed two new handles and seven new heads! I suppose that the modular construction of PCs leaves them open to the same sort of claim. Over the years you can put in a new display card here, a replacement disk drive there, and maybe even a new motherboard in the fullness of time. Five or six years later the computer will still be going strong, and will probably have a specification well above that of the original machine, but the case might be the only survivor from the original hardware!

The PC's modular method of construction aids the DIY repairer. Even if you can not mend the particular item that is faulty, then it can instead be completely replaced. This might seem to be a wasteful approach, and to an extent I suppose that it is. Being realistic about modern electronics in general, current production processes are so efficient that many pieces of equipment can now be produced at very low cost. Repairing equipment can take a lot of man hours from highly skilled (and well paid) service engineers, making it a costly process. Modern production processes are designed to make the manufacture of equipment as cheap as possible, with servicing usually being of only secondary importance. This makes fitting replacement parts on some circuit boards quite difficult.

Obviously each case has to be assessed on its own merits. Throwing away a high capacity hard disk drive that has become faulty just outside the guarantee period and replacing it will a new one would not be a cost effective way of handling the problem. At the other extreme, something like a parallel printer port card that has become faulty after several years use is probably not worth repairing. It would only cost a few pounds to replace it with a new one.

There is a big incentive to undertake DIY repairs. The cost of professional repairs on PCs can be quite high, with the minimum fee sometimes being higher than the cost of any one of an average PCs component parts. Carriage costs to and from the service centre can be high, as can calling in an engineer to provide on-site maintenance. While I would not advocate prodding around inside expensive computer

Fig.2.3 Hard copy printed at 300 d.p.i. on an ink-jet printer. Even the smallest text (6 point) is quite readable and neat

they produce is predominantly from the mechanisms that drive the printhead and feed the paper through. This contrasts with most dot-matrix printers where the printhead is very noisy, and drowns-out the sound from the rest of the printer.

The speed of ink-jet printers is generally quite high, being at least as good as the fastest dot-matrix types. The printing speeds for ink-jet and dot-matrix printers are normally quoted in terms of characters per second (or just "cps" for short). These speeds need to be taken with the proverbial "pinch of salt", and are often rather optimistic assessments of the printing speeds. They are usually accurate, but are the speeds obtained under favourable operating conditions that may never be met in real life.

Anyway, they are the speeds obtained when printing plain text, and have little bearing on the print speeds obtained when printing out pages using the graphics mode to obtain large text, fancy fonts, or whatever. With this method of printing the speed is often governed more by the speed at which the computer and software operate, than by the speed of the printer. When printing simple text it is the printer's built-in microprocessor that does most of the work, but this integral "intelligence" is largely bypassed when printing pages in the graphics mode. The computer and d.t.p. program have to work out each page dot-by-dot, which takes a great deal of calculating. In d.t.p. applications the only certain way of finding the print speed is to produce a few example pages and make a note of the times taken. This can vary enormously from one page to another, depending on their complexity. Masses of small text and (or) intricate graphics generally produce lengthened print times.

A minor disadvantage of ink-jet printers is that they are more costly to run than dot-matrix printers, although they actually compare quite favourably with high quality printers such as laser types. In many ways they are more comparable to laser printers than to dot-matrix types, and their running costs could reasonably be regarded as fairly average. Some ink-jet printers will only work properly with a special paper that has an absorbent coating. However, many recent types will operate perfectly well with ordinary typewriter, laser, or copier paper, and (somewhat ironically) must not be used with ink-jet paper! Apart from the increased convenience and versatility, this helps to keep down the running costs of these printers as ink-jet paper is relatively expensive.

Ink-jet printer ink is not usually waterproof, which makes these printers unsuitable for certain applications (such as producing legal documents), but does not prevent them from being used successfully in most d.t.p. applications. Ink-jet printers, being a non-impact type, can not be used with carbon paper to produce multiple copies. This is not something that is normally done when producing d.t.p. printouts, and does not really detract from their usefulness in d.t.p. applications.

Figure 2.3 shows a sample printout made using an ink-jet printer at a resolution of 300 dots per inch. Most laser printers (see below) produce an output of similar quality.

Laser Printers

Laser printers, with the exceptions of a few up-market types, all seem to operate at 300 dots per inch. Like ink-jet printers, they use a non-impact printing process with small and well formed dots. This gives excellent print quality that is adequate for all but the most demanding d.t.p. applications. They are based on photocopier technology – a factor which has tended to make them quite large and costly in the past. In recent times some smaller, lighter, and less expensive laser printers of good quality have been produced. At one time they were something that would only be found in an up-market d.t.p. system, but they are not quite the "luxury" item that they once were. They are still very much more expensive than dot-matrix printers though, and are also substantially more costly than the better ink-jet machines. You need to be fairly heavily into d.t.p. for the cost of one of these printers to be fully justifiable.

You may sometimes encounter references to LCD (liquid crystal display) and LED (light emitting diode) printers. These are basically similar to laser printers, but instead of using a scanning laser beam to produce the image, they use either a liquid crystal device plus a light source, or an array of light emitting diodes. As far as the user is concerned, it probably makes little difference which method is used to produce the image. Results are much the same with any of these printers, and they are much the same in use.

Apart from the high quality of the printing, laser printers have the advantage of very fast printing speeds. The speed of laser printers is normally quoted as pages per minute rather than characters per second. This is because they are fed with complete pages which are then printed in one go, rather than doing things one character at a time. A drawback of this approach is that it can take as long to print a largely blank page as it takes to produce one that is filled with text and complex graphics.

Most laser printers operate at around eight pages per minute. Note though, that this is with multiple copies of the same page being printed. The print speed is likely to be somewhat less when printing one copy at a time of several different pages. Bear in mind also, that with complex d.t.p. pages the time taken for the computer to work out the right data to send to the printer can take a significant time. This can result in a very fast printer not actually producing completed pages much faster than one which operates at a much more modest speed. This is something that depends to a large extent on the particular computer and software you use, but it does mean that fast printers sometimes fail to live up to expectations when used in d.t.p. applications.

Their speed and high print quality makes laser printers very desirable for d.t.p. work, but they are not totally without disadvantages. There are a couple of minor ones in that there is a characteristic smell produced by these printers which many people seem to find unpleasant. These printers often have cooling fans which can be a bit noisy, although probably much less so than the hard disk drives which are fitted to many computers these days.

Most types of printer produce the pages a bit at a time, as the data is received from the computer. This requires the printer to have little or no memory, as the data is used almost immediately it is received. The situation is different with laser printers where they must be fed with a full description of each page before it can be printed. This necessitates a large amount of memory to store all the data until it is ready to be used.

Most laser printers are supplied with about 512 kilobytes ("K") of memory, which is sufficient to permit a full page of ordinary text to be produced. Complex pages, particularly full pages of graphics, require more memory than this.

Typically, an extra megabyte (1024 kilobytes) will be needed in order to produce full pages of graphics, and in some circumstances even more memory than this might be needed in order to produce everything you require. Memory chip prices have fallen back from the very high prices of a few years ago, but such a large amount of memory is still far from cheap. This means that for d.t.p. use a memory upgrade will usually be required, which makes an already quite expensive type of printer even more costly. Always keep this point in mind when looking at laser printer prices.

The relatively high cost of these machines has already been mentioned, as has the large size of some models. The running costs are also relatively high. New cartridges of toner powder are not needed very often, but are quite expensive when they do have to be purchased. The drum on which the initial image is laid down has a finite life and needs periodic replacement. Most models require servicing by a trained engineer from time to time, in addition to servicing of any faults that might occur during the printer's lifetime. The latter is usually very long indeed (typically a few hundred thousand pages of printing), which to a large extent offsets the high initial cost and the running costs. However, this is only the case if the printer will receive a great deal of use. Otherwise it is likely to become obsolete before it has produced more than a small percentage of its quota of pages. One of the better ink-jet printers might be a better choice if you are only going to print about two thousand pages a year or less.

A point worth mentioning is that laser printers generally only print on paper up to A4 size. No reasonably low cost types seem to be able to handle the larger paper sizes that can be accommodated by the wide carriage dot-matrix printers, and some ink-jet types. Obviously A4 paper is large enough for most requirements, but it would presumably render ordinary laser printers unusable in some d.t.p. applications.

Compatibility with the d.t.p. program is something that has to be considered with any printer, including laser types. Most laser printers seem to offer a mode in which they emulate one of the Hewlett Packard "LaserJet" printers, and it is usually a "LaserJet II" emulation that is offered these days. Provided this emulation operates properly, it should ensure compatibility with practically any d.t.p. program, plus drawing programs of all types, word processors, etc. Some laser printers offer emulations of other printers, such as one of the Epson nine pin dot-matrix machines. One point to keep in mind with this sort of thing is that the emulation might be a text only type, and may no· work at all with most d.t.p. programs.

Another point to bear in mind is that even if the emulation does include graphics capabilities, the graphics quality produced will almost certainly be something roughly comparable to the emulated printer. This means that using something like a nine pin dot-matrix printer emulation will provide a print quality that is far short of the maximum quality available from the laser printer. In a d.t.p. context it is only worthwhile using an emulation that provides the full 300 dots per inch resolution of the printer.

Most of the more expensive laser printers are equipped to use "PostScript", or have a "PostScript" emultion mode. PostScript is a page description language, and it is a means by which the pages can be described to the printer without the computer having to control things on a dot-by-dot basis. It operates more on the basis of describing the page in terms of (say) a circle of a certain size at a specified position on the page, or a text string in a certain font, style, size and position. This is a rather more complicated method of handling things, but it does have its advantages.

First and foremost, the resolution is limited by the printing device, not by the software or any other factors. The quality obtained will therefore be as high as the printer can produce, whether it is a simple low resolution device or a super-high resolution printing machine costing many thousands of pounds. Another point in its favour is that it is relatively fast, even when complex pages are being produced.

It is worth noting that with some software the full capabilities of the program can only be realised if it is used with a "PostScript" output device. The reason for this is that with "PostScript" the printer contains a powerful microcomputer which works out the page on a dot-by-dot basis. This greatly reduces the amount of calculating that the main computer and the d.t.p. program must undertake (and speeds up the rate at which the correct matrix of dots for the page is worked out). This enables the software to handle things that would otherwise be beyond its capabilities. This includes such things as a greater range of text size (particularly large fonts), and complex fill patterns in the graphics.

Not all programs provide a greater range of facilities with "PostScript" output devices, but this is not exactly a rarity amongst the more up-market d.t.p. and graphics software. It is worth mentioning that the facilities offered by many d.t.p. and graphics programs varies somewhat depending on which particular printer is used, due to differences in the facilities offered by various printers.

"PostScript" is a desirable feature, but it is one that still costs quite a lot extra. This is inevitable, as it necessitates the inclusion of a substantial mount of extra hardware and software in the printer. If you can afford it, and you will be producing complex pages, then "PostScript" will probably prove to be well worth the additional cost.

With some computers there is a low cost route to "PostScript" in the form of programs that will take a "PostScript" disk file, and process it to produce the appropriate output for a range of printers. This enables "PostScript" to be used with dot-matrix and ink-jet printers, as well as with laser types which do not have it built-in. Of course, using "PostScript" with a relatively low resolution printer does not result in it producing high resolution output. You simply get the normal resolution of the printer, but possibly with facilities that would not be available with the printer driven direct from the d.t.p. program with its standard driver.

Although this method may seem to be an ideal one, saving a lot of money, it does have some drawbacks. One is that this method is not applicable to all computers, since suitable software is not available for some machines. It is something that is really only a practical proposition on fairly powerful computers. Even using a fairly up-market computer, the time taken for pages to be calculated can be quite long, making it impractical where large numbers of pages must be printed out. Finally, the implementation of "PostScript" might be less than complete, rendering some features of the software unusable. Where these limitations are acceptable, this software method represents a very good way of handling things.

Colour Printers

High quality colour printing requires expensive equipment, usually costing several thousands of pounds or more. There are some relatively low cost colour printers, but there is only a limited choice at present. The cheapest option is to use a colour ribbon in a dot-matrix printer. In most cases this simply changes the print from black to an alternative colour, with no mulit-colour capability being provided. Some dot-matrix printers can take special multi-colour ribbons which do provide several different print colours. The available palette is usually pretty limited though, with a maximum of about eight different colours being typical.

Thermal colour printers usually offer a much greater range of colours. These vary somewhat in the manner in which the print is produced, but they are usually based on a thick waxy ink on a ribbon or in reservoirs, with a heat being used to melt the ink so that it impregnates the paper. The cost of these printers varies enormously, as does the print quality. The ones at low prices normally have limited resolutions and might not produce strong saturated colours. With any colour printer it is a good idea to get some sample printouts to ascertain whether or not results are up to the standards you require. With any low cost colour printer this is especially important.

Probably the most popular low cost colour printers at present are the ink-jet types. The Hewlett Packard "PaintJet" is probably the nearest thing to a "standard" colour printer. This operates much like an ordinary ink-jet printer, but it has three colours of ink in the cartridge. In fact the "PaintJet" has a three-colour cartridge plus an ordinary black type. The latter is used when printing in black, and is also brought into action in place of the colour cartridge if the latter would use all three colours at the same strength. Different colours are produced by using the three primary colours in different strengths in dither patterns, and by adding black where necessary in order to give darker shades of the basic colours. This gives a useful range of a few hundred colours.

Provided they are used with suitable paper (which usually means special ink-jet paper or film in the case of these colour ink-jet printers), the colours produced are normally quite strong, but some of the available colours might not look too convincing. The resolution obviously varies from one printer to another, but in the case of the "PaintJet" it is comparable to twenty-four pin dot-matrix machines at 180 dots to the inch horizontally and vertically. The subjective quality is generally a bit better than that from twenty-four pin dot-matrix machines, presumably because the ink-jet printers do not use an impact process.

Using colour can help to give more professional looking results, and even using a very limited range of colours can give results that seem much better than a black and white equivalent. The difference is likely to be most noticeable on documents that contain a lot of graphics, almost regardless of the type of illustration used. Probably business graphics benefit the most, and apart from looking prettier, intelligent use of colour can make them easier to assess quickly. However, even something like technical drawings and illustrations can benefit greatly from the sensible use of colour. Colour printers are less expensive than they once were, but are still significantly more costly than monochrome types having a comparable resolution and print quality. Before buying a colour printer you should examine the running costs very carefully. These can be very much higher than for black and white printers, especially where large blocks of solid colour are involved.

Probably the main point to watch when selecting a colour printer is that of compatibility with the software. Most d.t.p. programs support one or two colour printers, but few have drivers for a large range of them. Make sure that your selected printer is properly supported in its colour mode, and that you will not end up with only black and white printouts! To stand a reasonable chance of full compatibility with the software you need to either choose a popular type, or one which can accurately emulate a popular colour printer such as the Hewlett Packard "PaintJet". One or more of these emulation modes now seems to be a common feature amongst colour printers. Alternatively, the printer might be supplied with driver software for use with some popular graphics packages.

The compatibility factor is something that needs to be carefully checked before buying a colour printer. Ideally you should actually see the printer in operation with your d.t.p. software and assess some sample printouts before purchasing the unit.

Plotters

Plotters are not used with d.t.p. programs, but can be used to produce graphics which can be added into d.t.p. programs using the paste-up method. A plotter could reasonably be regarded as a sort of mechanical draughtsman which draws on the paper using a pen. Various types of pen can be used, such as fibre-tip, technical, and ball-point types. Some plotters can even use a special pencil.

There is an important difference between plotters and most other forms of hard copy device in that they do not operate on the basis of producing the image from a matrix of dots. If a line is needed from point "A" to point "B", then a plotter does not use a series of dots to produce the line. Instead it simply draws the line, much as a human artist or draughtsman would produce the line. If a solid block is needed, the appropriate area is filled in using a number of lines side-by-side. This makes plotters well suited to some types of graphics, but of little use with other types.

Plotters are probably at their best with line drawings, such as most technical drawings and diagrams, and some types of technical illustration. In this context they would normally be used with technical pens drawing onto tracing paper. They also work well with most business graphics programs, giving multi-colour output if they are used with fibre-tip pens of various colours (or possibly with technical pens filled with inks of different colours). When used with plotter paper, which is very high quality paper having a smooth, semi-shiny surface, superb results can be obtained using coloured fibre-tip pens. Charts such as bar types look almost as though they have been produced using a high quality colour printing process.

Plotters are not very good for use with paint programs, due to the very different ways in which plotters and this type of software handle graphics. Paint programs work on a pixel basis, which is comparable to the way dot-matrix, ink-jet, and laser printers operate. In other words, the image is made up from many thousands of dots. Plotters do not work on a pixel basis, but converting pixel graphics into equivalent plotter commands is not a particularly difficult process. Despite this, few (if any) paint programs actually support any pen plotters. The probable reason for this is that the plotter would have to fill in, one-by-one, what would probably be between 100,000 and 1,000,000 little blocks of colour, which would take a very long time! Although plotters are potentially capable of producing very good quality hard copy from paint programs, in practice this combination is probably not a practical proposition.

The resolutions of plotters are mostly very high. Strictly speaking the resolution should be given in terms of step size (i.e. the minimum distance at a time that the pen can be moved vertically or horizontally) and not in terms of dots per inch. However, the quality obtained with a given step size is much the same that a printer gives with the same resolution in dots per inch, making comparisons very easy. Most plotters operate at between about 500 and 2000 steps to the inch, giving a resolution that is equivalent to about 500 to 2000 dots per inch. This is obviously better than most good quality ink-jet printers and laser printers. In fact many plotters now compare quite well with very high quality printing machines in this respect.

The quality of graphics produced by plotters is very high indeed. Plotted results are almost certainly neater and more accurate than any human draughtsman could manage by hand. This could give the impression that plotters will produce good quality drawings that are small but intricate. In practice this is not usually the case. With resolution figures you need to bear in mind that the dot size/pen width is just as important as the dots per inch/step size. At one time it was possible to obtain plotter pens down to 0.01 millimetres, which is roughly comparable to the dot size of 300 dots per inch printers. Plotter pens as fine as this are very easily broken, and no longer seem to be made. The minimum pen width now is about 0.2 millimetres for technical pens, or 0.3 millimetres for fibre-tip types.

This puts definite limitations on the intricacy that can be handled. In particular, in order to keep any text on the drawing readable, it is often necessary to plot the drawing quite large. Where small, highly detailed drawings are required, they will probably have to be plotted twice actual size and then reduced using a photocopier or a photographic reducing technique. This adds a stage to the process, but should give final artwork of the highest quality.

Chapter 3

FONTS

A font is a collection of characters in a particular size, style and typeface. If you change any of these, you have a different font. Selection of fonts, more than any other factor, will influence the appearance and effectiveness of your finished documents.

To take the factors which define a font one-by-one, the collection of characters is termed the "character set". Exactly what characters appear in the set, and in what order, is determined principally by the d.t.p. program you are using, and secondarily by the particular font. Most fonts for a particular program will contain the same characters, but special fonts, such as symbols and "Dingbats" will use a different (often unique) set of characters. Programs may support more than one standard character set. Ventura, for example, can use the Ventura International Character Set or the Ventura U.S. Character Set, which has fewer characters in it.

The size of a font is given in "points". Each point is approximately equal to 1/72 of an inch. A 12-point character is therefore 1/6 of an inch high. This size refers to the height of a normal capital letter. However, it is normal for the sizes of fonts as given for d.t.p. purposes to include the inter-line spacing, or "leading" (pronounced like the metal), so the actual height of the characters will normally be less than the nominal point size. The range of point sizes you can use will be set primarily by the d.t.p. program, and secondarily by the printer, as will the increments in which you can specify sizes. For most d.t.p. programs the smallest size you can use is 6-point. For dot-matrix printers (including impact and ink-jet types) the largest size may be 60-, 72- or 96-point, depending on printer and program. For laser printers using PostScript, the maximum size is usually 200-point. With dot-matrix printers you can only specify sizes in full points normally. With some programs, you can specify PostScript sizes in fractions of points.

Style and typeface are sometimes confused. Style means whether the letters are normal (called roman), italic, or bold. Other variations are possible, such as bold italic, light, outline, black, and so on. Light, normal, black, and bold are referred to as the "weight" of a typeface. Some other styles provided in conventional metal fonts, and in phototypesetting, such as reverse italics, are not normally found in d.t.p. Though you can have separate fonts for each style, it is not always necessary to do so. Most d.t.p. programs can generate an italic or bold style from the normal roman typeface, though this will not be quite the same as the "real thing" (see Figures 3.1 and 3.2). Not all typefaces will be found in all styles. Zapf Chancery, for instance, normally only comes in normal-weight italic.

The typeface is the aspect of the font which someone has designed. It gives the font its overall character and appearance. Over the course of the centuries since printing was invented, the number of typefaces designed runs into the tens of thousands. Of these, a few dozen are available in forms suitable for d.t.p. Typefaces have names which may be simply descriptive, or may be quite romantic. Probably the best-known typefaces, and the ones most commonly supplied with d.t.p. programs, are Helvetica, designed in 1957 by Max Meidinger, and Times Roman, designed for the Times newpaper around 1931/2. Variations on Helvetica include the Bitstream Fontware Swiss face (also supplied with GEM applications), and the GST Typografica Sans face. Variations on Times include the Bitstream Fontware Dutch face and the Typografica Serif face.

Devices and Font Types

Whilst fonts were made of typemetal, the above details were sufficient to describe a font fully. Within d.t.p., however, it is also necessary to specify the device for which the font is designed, be it a printer or a screen. Printer fonts will differ depending on the resolution which the printer can produce, and where the fonts are to be stored before use, either in the computer only, in the printer only, or at some stage transferred from computer to printer. The situation with screen fonts is simpler, as they only ever need to be stored in the computer.

With dot-matrix and ink-jet printers, and some laser printers, each page of output is produced in memory (this may include "slave files" on disk) and then sent to the printer as a "graphics dump", meaning that the computer directly controls each pin, nozzle or laser pulse during the printing operation. In this case, the fonts are always stored in the computer, and will be in a file form suitable for the d.t.p. program. Fonts of this type are termed "bit-maps", because each file contains maps or patterns of the dots which go to make up each character. This type of font allows the greatest flexibility (except as regards size), as during page generation the program can, if required, manipulate the bit-maps to alter the character style.

With some laser printers, the font files are stored in the computer in a form essentially similar to bit-maps, that is, as patterns of dots, but instead of each page being generated in the computer, the fonts to be used are down-loaded at the start of printing into memory within the printer. The page is then created within the printer from instructions sent from the computer. The Hewlett Packard LaserJet printers using the H-P Page Compilation Language (PCL) are the best-known examples of this. This method of printing is inherently less flexible than page production in the computer, but may be quicker as the fonts only need to be down-loaded once for each printing session. Fonts of this type are called "soft fonts", as distinct from the fonts built in to the printer, which are presumably hard fonts, though this term is not used.

The third possible variant is the use of a Page Compilation Language, of which Adobe PostScript is the best known, and the industry standard. It is used by some laser printers (for example the Apple

Chocolate eclairs

Chocolate eclairs

Chocolate eclairs

Chocolate eclairs

Chocolate eclairs

Chocolate eclairs

Chocolate eclairs

Chocolate eclairs

Chocolate eclairs

Chocolate eclairs

Chocolate eclairs

Chocolate eclairs

Chocolate eclairs

Chocolate eclairs

Chocolate eclairs

Chocolate eclairs

Fig. 3.1 Program-generated italic fonts

Chocolate eclairs

Chocolate eclairs

Chocolate eclairs

Chocolate eclairs

Chocolate eclairs

Chocolate eclairs

Chocolate eclairs

Chocolate eclairs

Chocolate eclairs

Chocolate eclairs

Chocolate eclairs

Chocolate eclairs

Chocolate eclairs

Chocolate eclairs

Chocolate eclairs

Chocolate eclairs

Fig. 3.2 True italic fonts

LaserWriters), and also by professional phototypesetters, such as those made by Linotronic. In PostScript printers, the fonts are stored in the printer as outlines, the shape of each character described as lines and curves independent of dimension. These outlines are scaled to any required size and filled in as required. These "outline fonts" are stored in the printer or phototypesetter, though it is also possible to down-load additional outlines to most PostScript printers, depending on the amount of memory available within the printer.

Hybrid systems also exist. For example, the driver supplied with Timeworks (U.K. version 1.2) for the H-P DeskJet printer can use a combination of down-loaded fonts and bit-mapped fonts. In this way, the small font sizes can be held in the printer, which speeds up printing, while the larger fonts, which could not fit into the memory available in the printer, are sent from the computer as graphics.

Screen fonts are an entirely separate thing to the printer fonts. If you want your printer fonts to be displayed correctly on screen, you will need matching screen fonts. Some d.t.p. programs require that you have exactly matching screen fonts in order to be able to use your printer fonts. Finesse is of this type. With other programs, if you do not have an exactly matching font, the nearest you have will be used instead. This may be either the same typeface in the nearest size (nearest smaller size with most programs), or failing that, the nearest available size in an alternate typeface. If no suitable alternative font can be found, nothing will be displayed on the screen, but the font will still print on the printer.

Most d.t.p. programs will display a document in (approximately) actual size, and also in double size to allow detail work, and half-size, to allow a full page to be displayed on-screen. To accommodate all these variations, you may need to have screen fonts in double and half the sizes of your printer fonts. You can keep the number of screen fonts you need within bounds by choosing a suitable progression of printer font sizes. For example, if you have printer fonts in 6-, 8-, 10-, 12-, 16-, 20- and 24-point, you only need screen fonts in these sizes and 32-, 40- and 48-point to cover all display sizes. (3-, 4- and 5-point screen fonts are not available, and would be too small to read. Text in these very small sizes is "greeked", displayed as grey shading.)

Adding Fonts

Desktop publishing programs normally come with only a restricted range of fonts, perhaps only two typefaces in half-a-dozen sizes, with perhaps some symbol or "bullet" fonts in addition. You can generally add further fonts, however.

Fonts can be purchased in "ready to run" form, where you buy a particular typeface in a particular size, but it is now much more normal to buy a font generator program, which uses outline fonts, the same in principal as those used in PostScript devices, and generates bit-map or soft fonts in any required size (within program and hardware limits) for any supported screen and/or printer.

The two best-known suppliers of font generators are Bitstream Fontware of Cambridge, Massachusetts, and GST, who supply the Typografica font generators and who, by coincidence, come from Cambridge, England. These font generators are similar in principle, but there are differences in practice.

Bitstream Fontware kits are normally supplied to work with one application only. If you need to make fonts for use with different applications, for example with Ventura and with a Windows application, you will need two kits. However, both kits may use the same outline fonts. Bitstream Fontware kits and additional outlines are quite expensive to buy, but are sometimes supplied with applications which use their fonts, for example Ventura and GEM applications. The kits will generate fonts for a wide variety of printers and screens. Fonts can be generated for down-loading to PostScript printers, but special outlines must be purchased to do this.

The Typografica font generator, on the other hand, can be used with a wide variety of applications, as well as screens and printers. When you buy a Typografica outline font, the generator program comes with it. You can also buy collections of fonts, at a cost saving compared with buying them individually. The GST product is considerably less expensive than the Bitstream, but cannot produce PostScript fonts.

The fonts from the two kits are a match for overall quality, but there are differences between them. In particular, the normal-weight Typografica fonts are a little lighter than the Bitstream equivalents. Which you prefer is really a matter of taste, but it does mean that it is not a good idea to mix fonts from the two sources in the same typeface. For example, with Timeworks PC, finished Bitstream fonts are supplied in 10- and 14-point. It would not be a good idea to use the Typografica kit to add a 12-point font, as if used together the difference in weight would be noticeable. You would need to replace all the fonts in this typeface with the Typografica ones, or use a Bitstream kit to generate the extra one. (NOTE: From Timeworks PC release 1.2 onward, Typografica fonts are supplied as standard in place of the standard GEM fonts.)

Though there are detail differences between them, using the two kits is similar in principle. It is important, firstly, to ensure the kit is correctly installed according to the instructions. The Bitstream kit in particular uses several subdirectories, and it is important that the various files used are placed correctly. Also, some files may be supplied on the distribution disks in a compressed form, and need to be decompressed as part of installation. It is not sufficient to simply copy all the files onto a hard disk. Though the Typografica kit can be used on a machine with two floppy disk drives, as d.t.p. is not really practical without a hard disk, it will be assumed here that a hard disk is in use. The Bitstream kits can only be used on a hard disk.

Once the kit is installed, and the font outlines added, font generation can begin. In the case of the Typografica kit, you must specify the application for which you wish to generate fonts. With both kits, you must specify which printer and screen you will be using, from those supported. If the actual printer you will be using is not listed, you may be able to select a compatible printer. For example, many 24-pin dot-matrix printers will use the same fonts as the Epson LQ series, as will the H-P PaintJet in graphics mode (i.e. not down-loading the fonts as "soft fonts", which are different). With Timeworks d.t.p. prior to version 1.2 (U.K.), which uses the H-P DeskJet as a graphics printer (rather than using the H-P PCL), LaserJet fonts can be used with the H-P DeskJet printer.

The next step is to select the typefaces in which you want to generate the fonts. With Typografica you can only generate fonts in one typeface at a time. With Bitstream, you can generate fonts in several typefaces in one session. For each typeface, you may have a choice of up to four styles, depending on what outlines are available, and have been installed. You specify which point sizes you wish to generate for each style in each typeface.

The Typografica kit allows the width of a font to be varied, from 25% to 200% of the normal width (i.e. from one-quarter to double). This is a facility which is best used sparingly, as fonts normally look best at their designed width. However, very wide or narrow fonts can be used to give impact to headlines, and sometimes, when text must be fitted into a document of limited size, using a font at 90% or 95% of normal width may give a more acceptable result than reducing the margins and gutters.

All the fonts you wish to generate must use the same character set. If you try to use an inappropriate character set, generation will be halted with error messages, as the kit will not be able to find appropriate outlines for some of the characters. Most straightforward alphanumeric fonts will use the same character set. This problem will normally only arise if you are generating symbol or Dingbat fonts. These need to be generated separately to alphanumeric fonts, and to each other.

In the case of the Typografica kit, you can choose to generate screen fonts or printer fonts only, or both in the same range of point sizes. The Bistream kit lets you specify screen and printer sizes separately. If you want to make extra screen sizes for the half and double size screen displays with the Typografica kit, these must be made in a separate operation. In such cases, you may prefer to keep screen font and printer font generation separate.

The range of sizes you can generate will depend on what your target application can use. The kits will not normally generate invalid sizes. However, the kits may impose limitations of their own depending on the screen and printer specified. For example, if you are generating screen fonts for a CGA display (640 x 200), the Bitstream kit will not let you generate screen fonts smaller than 10-point. In a way, this is sensible, as even 10-point fonts are difficult to read at this resolution, and smaller sizes are just smudges. However, there are advantages to being able to display such small sizes as individual characters, and the Typografica kit will generate screen fonts down to 6-point for all screens.

Font generation takes a considerable time, especially if you are generating large sizes, or producing a lot of fonts in one go. When you have specified all the sizes you wish to make, the kits will give you an estimate of how long the operation will take. In the Authors' experience, these estimates are reasonably accurate, the Bitstream kit being perhaps a bit optimistic. An advantage of the Bitstream kit is that it also tells you if you have sufficient disk space to take the finished fonts.

The generator kits will normally place the fonts directly into the appropriate subdirectories for your application. The kits are normally set up to use the default directories, for example the \VENTURA directory for Ventura DTP, or the \GEMAPPS\ FONTS directory for Timeworks DTP or Finesse. If you have your applications installed in a non-standard way, or you want to direct the font files elsewhere (perhaps onto floppy disks), you may need to alter the kit setup.

When producing full sets of fonts, the time taken can easily be half an hour to an hour, so this is a job where you need to set the computer going, and then go away and do something else until it has finished. The generator programs are quite robust and not inclined to crash, so this is quite safe. The Bitstream kit does have a stop in it, but this usually occurs, if it is going to, at the time-estimate stage, where it sometimes crashes with a "Division by zero" error. The cause seems to be trying to generate too many fonts in one go.

You do need to be sure the kit is actually generating the fonts before leaving it. Problems can arise if you are directing the finished fonts to floppy disk. Even if you have a hard disk, you may want to store most of your fonts on floppies, and just load the ones for current use onto your hard disk, in which case it can be a good idea to generate them directly onto the floppies. If you do this, the kit is likely to give a message to insert the disk and "Press any key" at some stage. Obviously you must get past this stage before leaving the computer to get on with it.

The kit may want to put screen and printer fonts on separate screen and printer disks, depending on which application the fonts are for. In such a case, you may need to be in attendance to change disks when required. Again, it may be better here to make screen and printer font generation completely separate operations.

Fonts are generated in a form which is immediately ready for use. However, your d.t.p. program may require further steps in order to be able to find and use the new fonts. This varies from application to application, and you should check the manuals supplied with both the program and the font generator kit for details. The kits may generate files in addition to the actual font files to enable your application to use the fonts. In particular, width files, also known as PFM or VFM files, may be produced. These files contain details of the widths of each character in each font file, and are used by the d.t.p. program when laying out pages. You must be careful not to accidentally delete or otherwise "lose" these files, or you may have to generate the fonts all over again.

Which Fonts to Generate

Being presented with a font generator kit is a bit like being presented with a very large box of chocolates, except that it is your computer which is likely to end up over-full. The temptation is to generate fonts in every typeface in a full range of sizes. If you do this for half-a-dozen typefaces, you will end up with easily a couple of hundred fonts, which can equally easily take up a couple of megabytes of hard disk space.

If you are heavily involved in d.t.p., and producing a wide variety of documents, you may need this many fonts, and be fully prepared to dedicate this amount of space to their storage. If you are less involved, perhaps only using d.t.p. for one or two types of document, or short of disk space, you will probably want to keep the number of fonts within reasonable limits.

As well as the disk space taken up, there may be other compelling reasons not to have too many font files. There may be a limit set by your d.t.p. program. It may have a set limit to the number of typefaces and/or a set limit to the number of point sizes it can use. Alternatively, the limit may be physical. With Timeworks DTP (version 1.12 for PC and compatibles), if the number of fonts is much over 200, or the size of the width file PUBLISH.WID goes much over 62,000 bytes, the program will not run. It stops with a message "Cannot find or open Width File", and the only cure is to delete some font files and run the application FONTWID to generate a new width file. With version 1.2 (U.K.), this problem has been solved, and the program will run with any number of fonts loaded. (There was a problem with early version 1.2 releases. If, when you come to print a document, you find that some of the large point size fonts do not print, and you either get nothing or the same typeface in a small point size, contact GST, who can supply a fix.)

Having too many fonts available may also slow down program operations. The program needs to refer to the font files for the pattern of each character in order to display it on the screen or printer. To reduce the number of disk accesses necessary, font files are stored in memory, but obviously, there is a limit to how many can be stored or "cached" in this way. The rest can only be referenced from disk, which takes much longer. With programs running under DOS, a further problem arises with the way files are stored. When a subdirectory is created, an area is set aside for recording the location of 63 files. When this number of files is exceeded, a further area must be set aside. Searching all these areas (called FATs) to find a particular file also takes time. Where fonts are stored in a subdirectory of their own, therefore, it is a good idea to try to keep the number of files to 63 or less. This may not be possible with programs like Ventura which do not keep fonts in their own subdirectory.

If you need to keep the number of font files down, there are many ways of doing it. The most obvious is to make sure you only have fonts which you need. However, you will need to do some experimenting with a variety of fonts to find out which are the essential ones.

Your equipment may make some fonts redundant. For example, there is little point having fonts smaller than 10-point if you are using a 9-pin dot-matrix printer, as the quality will be unacceptable. For the same reason, it is not worth going below 8-point with a 150 or 180 d.p.i. printer. However, small size fonts use up much less space than large point sizes, and greater savings can be made by eliminating unused headline-size fonts.

As stated earlier, most d.t.p. programs can generate bold and italic styles from a normal-weight roman font, so the number of fonts can be kept down by not generating style variants, but you need to check what your d.t.p. program can do. Given a normal roman style font, Timeworks DTP can generate bold, italic, and bold italic styles. Ventura will generate bold and italic, but not bold italic. However, it can generate a bold italic from a bold roman font.

The program-generated style variants will not be the same as the fonts generated by the kits. The differences between a roman and an italic font are more than just a slant to the letters. The actual form of the characters is different. This is largely because the roman forms are derived from inscriptions carved in stone, whereas italic forms are derived from calligraphy and handwriting. The different forms are particularly noticeable in lower-case letters, especially "a", "e", "i", "l", and "t" (as shown in Figures 3.1 and 3.2).

When a d.t.p. program generates an italic style from a roman font, it cannot alter the letter forms. All it does is slant the letters. To be pedantic, it produces an oblique, rather than italic, form. The second limitation is that it gives an equal amount of obliqueing to all typefaces, whereas when proper italic fonts are generated, the amount of obliqueing will be determined by the typeface designer to give the character he intends, and will therefore vary from typeface to typeface.

Similar problems can arise with emboldening by the d.t.p. program. The degree of emboldening will be fixed for all fonts, and will also be proportional to the original weight of the font. If the normal font is on the light side to start with, the degree of emboldening will be less, and the result may be weak in effect. This can occur with some of the Typografica fonts. The Avant Garde font is quite a light typeface, but the kit-generated bold form is much bolder, giving a very noticeable difference between the two. If the normal weight style is emboldened by a d.t.p. program, the added weight is not very great, so that it is only obviously a bold face if you can compare it directly with the normal version.

The program-generated styles can be satisfactory if you do not make much use of bold or italic forms, but if you really care about your typesetting, you are likely to want to use the proper fonts, especially once you have been able to compare the two. A compromise, possible only with those programs which do not insist on matching screen and printer fonts, is to generate all the styles in printer fonts, but only to generate screen fonts in normal Roman, as screen appearance does not affect the finished document. Of course, the biggest savings in numbers of fonts are to be made by limiting the number of typefaces you use.

Using Fonts in Documents

The choice of which, and how many, fonts must always be compromise. On the one hand, if you use too many different fonts, the effect will be cheap and overdone, like a spiv's advertisement. On the other hand, if you restrict yourself too much, the effect can be dull and unattractive, even boring.

In general, in something like an advertisement, where there is little incentive to read the material presented, you need to use a greater variety of typefaces and styles, to attract and hold the attention. On the other hand, with material which is intrinsically interesting, fewer styles can be used, and this adds dignity. In things like high-quality literature and journalism, and also technical publications, a single typeface may be used, in perhaps only two or three sizes, with a simple, formal page layout. This adds an air of dignity and authority.

Much can be learned from a study of the different styles used in advertisements, both the typefaces used and the general layout of the material. The style clearly indicates the market at which the advertisement is aimed. For example, cheap electrical goods are sold with a style which uses lots of different fonts, in sizes from large bold headings to very small print (giving the APR for credit terms!). Layouts are irregular, and text often angled, to give an air of urgency. At the other end of the market, luxury cars are sold with a style which is more formal, with a large photograph being the main feature. Text is formally laid out, in a typeface chosen to suit the projected personality of the car, often using no more than two fonts, to convey an atmosphere of quality and reliability.

It is also interesting to observe that the greatest "con-merchants" of all, the pseudo-religious organisations, use a style of advertisement which closely mimics editorial material. This often causes editors to insist on the word "advertisement" being placed prominently at the top. This style is designed to try to fool readers into taking seriously material which is invariably complete balderdash.

Typefaces

Typefaces come in two main categories. The largest group consists of those typefaces which have small, decorative extensions, called "serifs", to the letter forms, and which are therefore called "serified" fonts. The other group consists of plain typefaces which do not have serifs, and which are called "sans serif", or just "sans", typefaces.

Most d.t.p. programs are supplied with one sans face and one serified face as a minimum, usually with a symbol or "bullet" font also included. Most usually, the sans face is one based on the Helvetica style. In Bitstream Fontware, this style is called "Swiss". The most common serified typeface is one based on Times Roman, called "Dutch" by Bitstream. The Typografica versions of these two faces are called Sans and Serif respectively. These two faces are justifiably popular, and can be used for a wide variety of purposes.

Typeface designs are subject to copyright. The quality of fonts supplied with d.t.p. programs does vary, and in general, those which are correctly licensed from the copyright holders are better (in some cases substantially so) than those which are not. It is therefore generally a good idea to choose fonts from ranges where at least some of the typefaces are correctly licensed. Both Bitstream and Typografica fall into this category. Some d.t.p. programs are supplied with a very wide range of styles and fonts, but the quality can leave a lot to be desired. The Authors have heard these referred to as "typefaeces", which has a certain wit to it. (Note however that some typefaces are in the public domain, and can be used by anyone.)

It is often said that serified typefaces are easier to read in body text than sans faces. This is perhaps because the serifs help to emphasise the horizontal direction of the text, easing scanning by the eye. However, not everyone agrees with this, and the Authors experience no difficulty in reading large blocks of Helvetica. Notwithstanding this, one very popular combination is to use the Times face for body text, and Helvetica for headlines. The opposite, Helvetica for body text and Times for headlines, is also used, but less common. Both these combinations give visual appeal, without losing dignity.

Other typefaces available tend to be more specific in application. Brief descriptions of the most generally available faces for d.t.p. are described here, with ideas on where they can best be used. The faces chosen are available from both Bitstream and Typografica, and are also the ones built-in to the Apple LaserWriter printer. This should not be taken as a complete list of the typefaces available.

ITC Avant Garde is an aggressively modern sans typeface, dating from as recently as 1970. It is a broad typeface, as the rounded letters, such as lower case a, e, and c are truly based on circles rather than ellipses. The form of the lower case "a" is more like the italic form than the usual Roman, and this can make it hard to distinguish from the lower case "o", especially in small point sizes printed on dot-matrix printers. Avant Garde is mostly used for advertisements, and for lettering on packaging, where a modern or futuristic appearance is intended. It can be difficult to read as body text, and also takes up more space than, for example, Helvetica, because of its breadth. It is perhaps at its best in point sizes of 14 and above. A combination of Avant Garde for headlines and Helvetica for body text will give documents which combine a clean, modern appearance with good legibility. (See Figure 3.3.)

ITC Bookman is, as the name suggests, a typeface intended for book production. It is a conservative design, perhaps even slightly old-fashioned, though this could be used to give documents a "period" appearance. It dates from around 1925. It is best used for body text, where it remains legible even in small point sizes, providing a printer of good resolution is used. The letter forms can be rather wide in headline sizes. The italic form is one of the most upright you will find. Bookman is usually used on its own, rather than in combination with other typefaces. (See Figure 3.4.)

Century Schoolbook is another typeface which is intended mostly for book production and body text. Despite dating from around 1895, it has quite a modern appearance. It was designed to provide easy legibility, which it does. The letters have large bodies with short ascenders and descenders, and the normal weight gives quite a black appearance. The bold form is very bold, and the italic quite strongly slanted. It is a good alternative to Times Roman for densely-set body text and, like ITC Bookman, normally used on its own rather than in combination with other faces. (See Figure 3.5.)

Courier (or Courier 10) is a typewriter face. It is a monospace typeface, which means all the letters occupy the same width. This means that wide letters like M and W have to be made rather narrow and squashed, whilst narrow letters like i and l have exaggerated serifs to make them artifically wider. In d.t.p., Courier is mostly used for tables and similar uses where it is desirable to have all the letters line up vertically. However, some d.t.p. programs will insist on trying to put extra space between the letters, and particularly, reduce or increase the space between words. This does rather reduce the usefulness of a monospace font. If you want to mimic typewriter output, 10-point will give 12 characters per inch, and 12-point 10 characters per inch, approximately. Courier will reproduce well on dot-matrix printers, even 9-pin types. (See Figure 3.6.)

Helvetica Narrow is just what the name suggests, a version of Helvetica in which the width of the letters is reduced in relation to their height. This allows more text to be fitted into a given space, but in body text sizes, the effect can be a bit cramped if there is a lot of text to read. The narrow form is perhaps best used for headlines, where the relatively greater height adds dignity, and the reduction of width allows longer headings without having to split them over two lines, which can be useful for subheadings in multiple-column layouts. Helvetica Narrow headings combined with normal Helvetica body text can work well, but it is not a good idea to combine the two types in the same point size. As with normal

Avant Garde

ITC Avant Garde is an aggressively modern sans typeface, dating from as recently as 1970. It is a broad typeface, as the rounded letters, such as lower case a, e, and c are truly based on circles rather than ellipses. The form of the lower case 'a' is more like the italic form than the usual roman, and this can make it hard to distinguish from the lower case 'o', especially in small point sizes printed on dot-matrix printers. Avant Garde is mostly used for advertisements, and for lettering on packaging, where a modern or futuristic appearance is intended. It can be difficult to read as body text, and also takes up more space than, for example, Helvetica, because of its breadth. It is perhaps at its best in point sizes of 14 and above. A combination of **Avant Garde for headlines** and **Helvetica for body text** will give documents which combine a clean, modern appearance with good legibility.

Fig. 3.3 Avant Garde and Helvetica fonts

Helvetica, the italic form is just an obliqued roman form, and so you may not find it worthwhile to generate them. In Bitstream Fontware this typeface is called Swiss Narrow, and in Typografica Sans Narrow. (See Figure 3.7.)

Palatino is a classically elegant typeface, designed by Hermann Zapf in 1949. It has tall letter forms, with long ascenders and descenders on the lower-case letters. There is quite strong modulation in the line widths of the letters, giving an effect like carving on stone. It is quite readable in body text, but the height of the letters also make it particularly good for headlines in large point sizes, where it combines grace and dignity. Palatino is much used for art books, books of photographs, and books of poetry, and also for quality magazines in these areas. The italic form is particularly beautiful. Palatino can be used on its own, for body text and headlines, but a combination of Palatino body text and Helvetica Narrow headlines also works well. Palatino really needs a printer of 300 d.p.i. or better resolution. Low resolution printers ruin the effect, at least in body-text sizes. The Typografica version of this font is called Palermo. (See Figure 3.8.)

Zapf Chancery is a very decorative typeface based on the Chancery Italic or Florentine calligraphic alphabet. It usually comes only in a normal weight italic form, though some d.t.p. programs will generate a bold variant from this. This face was somewhat over-used in the early days of d.t.p. You could always tell the Macintosh-prepared advertisements from the shaded boxes with rounded corners and the Zapf Chancery font! This typeface is therefore now something of a cliché, but can still be useful for advertisements, notices, signs and invitations, and is sometimes used in place of an italic version of a standard typeface for picture captioning. It is not really suitable for body text, where it is fussy and

ITC BOOKMAN

ITC Bookman is, as the name suggests, a typeface intended for book production. It is a conservative design, perhaps even slightly old-fashioned, though this could be used to give documents a 'period' appearance. It dates from around 1925. It is best used for body text, where it remains legible even in small point sizes, providing a printer of good resolution is used. The letter forms can be rather wide in headline sizes. The *italic form* is one of the most upright you will find. Bookman is usually used on its own, rather than in combination with other typefaces.

Fig. 3.4 ITC Bookman font

difficult to read, and can look a bit odd in large point sizes. It is best used between 14 and 24 points. (See Figure 3.9.)

Symbols, Bullets and Dingbats

In addition to the normal alphanumeric fonts, there are special fonts which include different characters. Symbols include such things as the mathematical symbols for plus, minus, multiply, divide and so on, and also such things as copyright and registered trade mark symbols. Bullets are characters like large dot, star, pointing hand, etc., which are placed at the beginning of a paragraph for emphasis. In magazines, they are also sometimes placed at the end of articles to indicate that there is no further carry over to following pages. Dingbats are decorative designs like rosettes, and also symbols like scissors, telephone, pointing hands, large ticks, and so on, which can be used for decorative purposes in documents. There may be some overlap between the contents of bullet character sets and Dingbat character sets.

Most of the contents of these character sets will not be shown on conventional keyboards. To use them you need to know which symbol corresponds to which conventional character. A chart may be provided with the font, or included in the d.t.p. program documentation where the font is "original equipment", or you may need to print one yourself. To access the special characters, you look up and type the corresponding normal character, and then change it to the special font. Some d.t.p. programs, for example Timeworks DTP, have a special bullet paragraph style which automatically puts your choice of bullet at the start of each paragraph tagged with this style.

Century Schoolbook

Century Schoolbook is another typeface which is intended mostly for book production and body text. Despite dating from around 1895, it has quite a modern appearance. It was designed to provide easy legibility, which it does. The letters have large bodies with short ascenders and descenders, and the normal weight gives quite a black appearance. The bold form is very bold, and the italic quite strongly slanted. It is a good alternative to Times Roman for densely-set body text and, like ITC Bookman, normally used on its own rather than in combination with other faces.

Fig. 3.5 Century Schoolbook font

Courier 10

Courier (or Courier 10) is a typewriter face. It is a monospace typeface, which means all the letters occupy the same width. This means that wide letters like M and W have to be made rather narrow and squashed, whilst narrow letters like i and l have exaggerated serifs to make them artificially wider. In DTP, Courier is mostly used for tables and similar uses where it is desirable to have all the letters line up vertically.

However, some DTP programs will insist on trying to put extra space between the letters, and, particularly, reduce or increase the space between words. This does rather reduce the usefulness of a monospace font. If you want to mimic typewriter output, 10-point will give 12 characters per inch, and 12-point 10 characters per inch, approximately.

Fig. 3.6 Courier font

HELVETICA NARROW

Helvetica Narrow is just what the name suggests, a version of Helvetica in which the width of the letters is reduced in relation to their height. This allows more text to be fitted into a given space, but in body text sizes, the effect can be a bit cramped if there is a lot of text to read. The narrow form is perhaps best used for headlines, where the relatively greater height adds dignity, and the reduction of width allows longer headings without having to split them over two lines, which can be useful for subheadings in multiple-column layouts.

Helvetica Narrow Headings

Helvetica Narrow headings combined with normal Helvetica body text can work well, but it is not a good idea to combine the two types in the same point size. As with normal Helvetica, the italic form is just an obliqued roman form, and so you may not find it worthwhile to generate specific italic fonts where your DTP program can generate them. In Bitstream Fontware this typeface is called Swiss Narrow, and in Typografica Sans Narrow.

Fig. 3.7 Helvetica Narrow font

Palatino

Palatino is a classically elegant typeface, designed by Hermann Zapf in 1949. It has tall letter forms, with long ascenders and descenders on the lower-case letters. There is quite stong modulation in the line widths of the letters, giving an effect like carving on stone. It is quite readable in body text, but the height of the letters also make it particularly good for headlines in large point sizes, where it combines grace and dignity. Palatino is much used for art books, books of photographs, and books of poetry, and also for quality magazines in these areas. The italic form is particularly beautiful.

Palatino and Sans Narrow.

Palatino can be used on its own, for body text and headlines, but a combination of Palatino body text and Helvetica Narrow headlines also works well. Palatino really needs a printer of 300 dpi or better resolution. Low resolution printers ruin the effect, at least in body-text sizes. The Typografica version of this font is called Palermo.

Fig. 3.8 Palatino font

Zapf Chancery

Zapf Chancery is a very decorative typeface base on the Chancery Italic or Florentine calligraphic alphabet. It comes only in a normal weight italic form, though some DTP programs will generate a bold variant from this. This face was somewhat over-used in the early days of DTP. You could always tell the Macintosh-prepared advertisements from the shaded boxes with rounded corners and the Zapf Chancery font! This typeface is therefore now something of a cliche, but can still be useful for advertisements, notices, signs and invitations, and is sometimes used in place of an italic version of a standard typeface for picture captioning. It is not really suitable for body text, where it is fussy and difficult to read, and can look a bit odd in large point sizes. It is best used between 14 and 24 points.

Fig. 3.9 Zapf Chancery font

Chapter 4
GRAPHICS

Obviously in much d.t.p. work graphics (diagrams, charts, etc.) are not essential, but there is something in the old adage which says that "a picture is worth a thousand words". Whether you are producing a club newsletter, business report, an advertisement, or practically anything, some pictures of one kind or another are almost certain to improve it. Apart from giving a less "dry" look to the finished product, pictures can make it much easier to get across the points you are trying to make. The type of graphics you will need to use varies greatly from one type of publication to another. A business report might require something like pie charts imported from a spreadsheet, a technical article would probably require some complex technical illustrations or diagrams, while an advertisement might benefit from some simple sketches of the products on sale.

In some cases it is photographs that are required. This is a subject that will not be covered here though. One method of using photographs is to scan them into a graphics program, and then after any necessary scaling or other modifications have been made, they are imported into the d.t.p. program. Except for the more sophisticated scanners, this will not give a particularly high standard of reproduction. Scanning is a subject that is covered in a separate chapter. In most cases it is probably best to simply use conventional paste-up methods to add photographs into their reserved areas of the pages.

Sources

If you need to add illustrations of some kind to a document, there may be a problem in obtaining suitable material. Many d.t.p. programs have drawing facilities, but these are usually very basic indeed. They are mainly just intended for such things as drawing frames around pieces of text, or the production of extremely basic diagrams. With most d.t.p. programs there is little likelihood of being able to produce even fairly simple illustrations with the drawing facilities built into the program. The drawings, charts, etc., must be originated elsewhere, and then imported into the d.t.p. program. It is only fair to point out that a few of the more simple d.t.p. programs have little or no facilities for importing graphics from other programs. These mostly have slightly better than normal integral drawing facilities, and you just have to do the best you can with these.

Alternatively, you might be able to reserve areas of the pages into which diagrams, etc., can be pasted on the printouts.

Business graphics are not likely to represent a major difficulty. In many cases the basic data will already be in a spreadsheet, or perhaps a similar program such as an accounting type, which will be capable of producing a range of graph types. In theory at any rate, it is just a matter of getting the spreadsheet (or whatever) to output the graphs or charts to a series of disk files which can be loaded into the d.t.p. program.

In the real world there are a number of potential problems. Firstly, not all programs that can handle business oriented data can produce graphs and charts. If your software can not do so, then a business graphics program will be needed in order to produce the illustrations. In fact practically any drawing program can be used to produce business graphics and charts, which in general are pretty basic. There are potential advantages in using a business graphics program though. Paint and CAD (computer aided drawing) are mostly quite complex to learn and use. If you are already using one of these to produce other types of illustration, and it can produce business charts, etc., quite easily, then there is obviously no point in obtaining a business graphics program.

If you do not already have software of this type, but will need to obtain some in order to produce some of the illustrations you will require, then it might be worthwhile holding back to see if this can produce the business charts, etc., as well. Probably in most cases where business graphics will be needed, these will be the only graphics that will be included in documents. A business graphics program is then the better choice as it is designed specifically for the production of the kinds of illustration you will need, making the process of producing them a relatively simple and straightforward one. You may even find that there is a graphics program that can read in data from your spreadsheet, database, or whatever, and produce the required charts largely automatically.

The facilities available in business graphics programs vary greatly from one program to another, with similar variations in their prices. In the past these programs have tended to offer little in the way of normal drawing facilities (for producing lines, circles, etc.). This rendered them of little use for anything other than producing standard business charts and graphs. Many of the programs currently on offer have better, but still rather limited, facilities of this type. However, they can mostly be used for something more than pie charts, bar charts, etc.

Most business graphics programs operate on the basis of offering several graph and chart types (pie chart, line graph, etc.). Most programs now include some 3D effect charts, such as 3D pie charts (Figure 4.1). These do not actually convey any more information than the normal two dimensional variety, but look somewhat more "professional". When using one of these programs, basically all you have to do is select the type of chart you require, answer a series of questions (to select the required text font, headings, etc.), and feed in the necessary data. You can often embellish the chart produced with additional labels, etc. With the more up-market programs you have a wide choice of text fonts and sizes, and can also add lines and other drawing elements to the chart or graph. You may even be able to produce simple flow charts, logos, and other simple illustrations. In some cases there is even a library of predrawn artwork which can be used in your illustrations.

3D PIE CHART

5 Segment Example

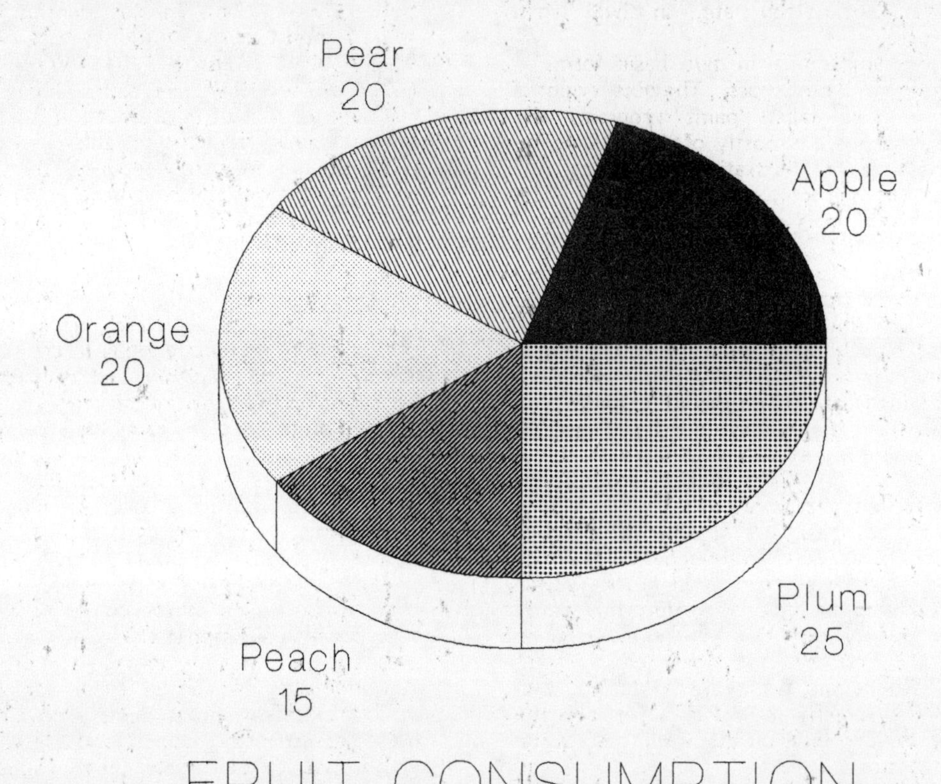

***Fig. 4.1** A 3D pie chart produced using Harvard Graphics Business graphics programs permit this type of thing to be produced very quickly*

Pixel Graphics

If you need to produce technical illustrations, sketches, non-business charts, diagrams, etc., then there are a wide range of drawing programs available which can handle these tasks. In some instances a business graphics program might still be the best choice. There are a lot of charts and graphs which are used to display statistical information, and are in many ways like business graphics, but which are not strictly speaking in this category. Business graphics programs will handle most charts of this type with few difficulties, as will spreadsheet programs that have a graphics capability.

Where the information is of a highly scientific or technical nature, it might be beyond the capabilities of a business graphics program or even a spreadsheet. There may then be no option but to use one of the specialist scientific/mathematical graphics programs. These are often something less than straightforward in use, but presumably anyone who needs to produce scientific graphs, etc., will understand the terminology, etc., involved when using these programs.

Drawing programs come in two basic forms – the vector and pixel based types. The pixel oriented programs are normally called "paint" programs. The vector based programs are mostly of the CAD (computer aided drafting) and illustration types.

Pixel based programs are the more simple type, and they work at the screen resolution. This is an important factor, since it places very definite limits on the resolution that can be obtained, and therefore limits the quality of the final output. This limitation on the quality of the final output can make pixel graphics unsuitable for some applications, but it may not matter in others. This really depends on the resolution obtained, and the type of graphics you will be producing. If you have a PC with a CGA colour screen operating at 320 x 200 pixels, this is unlikely to give a good quality final printout unless the drawing is reproduced quite small.

Maximum output quality is obtained with a one-to-one relationship between the screen pixels and the dots of the output device. Using an output device capable of 300 dots per inch resolution, this would give optimum quality with the drawing just over an inch wide by 0.66 inches high! Higher screen resolutions give greater scope, and with an 800 x 600 pixel super VGA screen, at 300 dots per inch the optimum size for the final output would be a more useful 2.66 inches by 2 inches.

It is not strictly accurate to say that drawings are limited to the same resolution as the display screen. It is possible to have a drawing that (in pixel terms) is larger than the screen, with the screen only showing part of it at any one time. Some paint programs do offer this over-size screen facility, but it is by no means a universal feature. In practice the amount of memory available usually limits the drawing size to something not that much larger than the screen size. With some paint programs part of the screen is taken up by menu bars, etc., effectively reducing the screen size. This does not normally reduce the drawing resolution very much though.

Paint programs are normally used for simple sketch type illustrations, although many can handle quite impressive looking multi-coloured "paintings" if that is what you need. They are not suitable for most technical illustrations, diagrams, etc., because their resolution is simply not adequate to carry all the necessary detail. Any graphics program is likely to take a certain amount of time and effort to master, but paint programs are probably the easiest type to learn. Much work with paint programs is done by simply drawing on the screen freehand using the mouse to control the on-screen "pen". Drawing freehand using a mouse is not quite as easy as you might think, and this aspect of paint programs can take some time to master. All paint programs seem to have good editing facilities so that it is reasonably easy to correct any mistakes you make.

Most paint programs can be made to operate with a digitising tablet, and it is then possible to use a pen-type drawing instrument instead of the puck (the digitising equivalent of a mouse). Even if the paint program has no support for a digitising tablet, many of these devices come complete with mouse emulation software. This enables them to be used with any program that has mouse support, which includes all the paint programs I have encountered. The tablet will probably operate in relative mode (like a mouse) rather than in absolute mode (which is the normal mode for digitising tablets). However, for a paint program either mode is perfectly suitable.

There is a definite advantage in using a pen-type tool for freehand drawing. It is the type of tool we have all used for drawing since we were toddlers, giving it an intuitive quality that is lacking when using a mouse type pointing device. Even so, it can still take a while to be completely accustomed to using one of these. It takes a while to get acclimatised to drawing on the digitising tablet with the results appearing on the screen of the monitor.

With most paint programs there are many drawing facilities in addition to simple freehand drawing. Special commands for drawing arcs, circles, polygons, etc., are normally included. There are usually options that permit enclosed areas to be filled with blocks of colours or even complex patterns. Text in various sizes and fonts can normally be added, and there may even be things such as various nib shapes that permit calligraphic effects to be obtained, and a "spray paint" facility that gives an effect much like painting using an aerosol spray can (Figure 4.2).

The more up-market paint programs have some quite sophisticated features, and are very capable if you are able to fully master them. I suppose that this is the major drawback of paint programs. If you have some artistic talent, it is not too difficult to learn to use a paint program effectively, and to produce the artwork that you require. On the other hand, if your artistic talents are strictly limited, you may be able to learn to use the program's facilities, but you may never produce anything more than doodles which are no use for the final product.

Another point to bear in mind if you intend to produce your own artwork is that it can be much more time consuming than you might expect. It is surprising how fast time passes when you are using one of these programs, even once you have become used to using the program. Producing your own illustrations with a paint program is only a practical

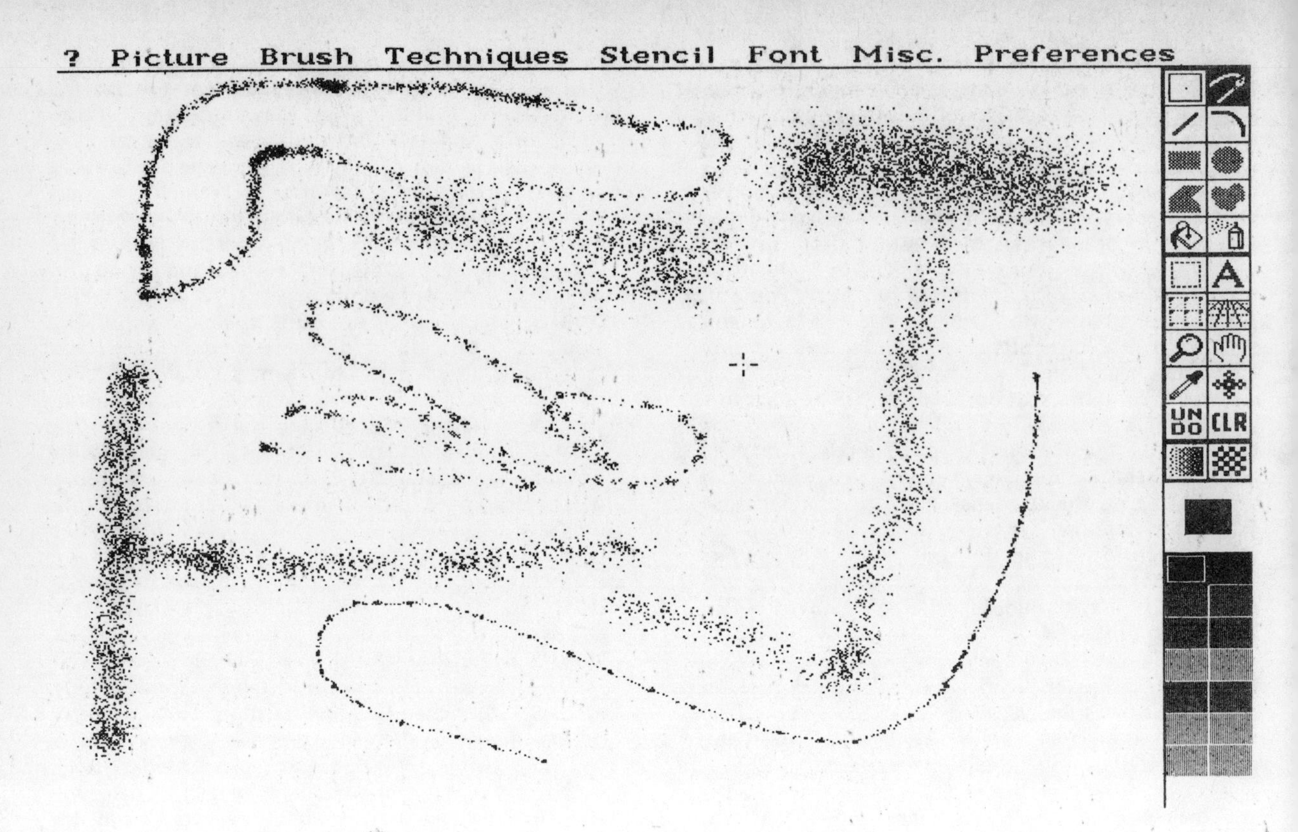

Fig. 4.2 Scribbling using the spray paint facility of Deluxe Paint II Enhanced. This is just one of several standard paint program drawing tools

proposition if you have plenty of time available to draw up the illustrations, or you only require some pretty simple drawings.

Clip-Art

If you do not have the necessary skills to produce your own artwork, there is an alternative in the form of clip-art. This is merely predrawn material covering almost every conceivable subject. The drawings are stored in files on floppy disks so that they can be loaded into suitable d.t.p. and paint programs. It is quite common for d.t.p. programs to have a certain amount of clip-art included as standard, and there is often further clip-art available as optional extras. There are also independent "third party" companies that produce clip-art for use with the popular d.t.p. programs.

The clip-art supplied with d.t.p. programs is usually of excellent quality, but the range of subjects covered is not likely to be vast. This reveals the main problem with clip-art. There must be an almost limitless range of subjects that d.t.p. users will require, and there is no way that even a very generous amount of sample clip-art can cover all requirements. In fact there is no way that a company with an extremely large catalogue of clip-art can cover all eventualities. Unless you can afford to have custom clip-art drawn up, which few d.t.p. users can seriously contemplate, you will probably need to compromise over the artwork from time to time. If you can not find exactly what you require, perhaps you can locate something that is just about close enough to your requirements. On the other hand, it is better to leave out illustrations altogether than to use artwork that is not really appropriate. Someone who has a paint program and the ability to draw up whatever artwork they need clearly have an enormous advantage over someone who is restricted to using clip-art.

It is perhaps worth mentioning that there is plenty of PD (public domain) and shareware clip-art available for some of the computers that are popular for d.t.p. Although PD and shareware software often tend to be grouped together as though they were exactly the same, they are actually totally different concepts. In both cases you pay what is usually only about £2.00 to £3.00 per disk to the supplier, but you are only paying for the disk itself plus a copying fee. In the case of PD software the author has decided not to claim copyright on his or her work, and it is available for anyone to use in any way they see fit, free of charge. This means that you are free to modify the material and use it as often as you like.

Shareware is a totally different concept, and is supplied on a "try before you buy" basis. Normally this type of software is in the form of a program which you try out over an evaluation period of up to about one month. If you decide to go on using the program you register your copy by sending the requested fee to the author. This fee is usually somewhat below the asking price for comparable commercial software. There may be some advantage in registering (apart from peace of mind for your honesty). This is often in the form of a proper manual to replace the on-disk operating instructions, plus perhaps a copy of a more advanced version of the program. In a clip-art context you get the items of clip-art on the disk, and you are required to register if you should decide to go ahead and actually use some of it in earnest. Whether you are expected to pay for the lot or only the items you actually use depends on the artist's conditions. You have to check these, which are to be found in a text file on the disk.

If you can find suitable clip-art in an appropriate format for your d.t.p. program, and at a price you can afford, then it offers a reasonably quick and straightforward solution to the problem. In practice you might find it difficult to satisfy all these criteria for all of your requirements. Possibly the best solution is to use clip-art where possible, but to resort to the do-it-yourself approach with a paint program when suitable clip-art can not be obtained.

Vector Graphics

With a pixel graphics system the drawing is stored in the computer's memory as a sort of map, with a small section of memory being used to indicate what is at each screen position, even if it is only black. Vector graphics programs are very different, and drawings are stored using a high resolution co-ordinate system. The resolution in which drawings are stored varies from one program to another, but it is generally about one hundred thousand by one hundred thousand or more. Many vector graphics programs can operate with co-ordinates of many millions on each axis. Such high resolution precludes having the drawing stored in memory as a pixel style bit map. Even for a monochrome display this would require many megabytes of memory.

Instead, the drawing is stored in memory as a list of drawing elements. A line would be stored in memory as three pieces of information, coded in a manner selected by the programmer. First there would be the code number for a line, then the co-ordinate for one end of the line, and finally the co-ordinate for the other end of the line. A circle would be coded in a similar fashion, with first the circle code number, then the co-ordinate for the centre of the circle, and finally a value indicating the diameter of the circle. Any drawing elements (arcs, text, etc.) can be coded and stored in memory in a similar fashion. In practice things might be more complex than this, with additional information such as line widths and layer numbers having to be included. However, this does not affect the basic way in which things are handled, it just means that more information for each element in a drawing has to be coded and stored in memory.

The advantage of this method is that it enables drawings to be stored with resolutions that are as high as the application demands, rather than having the screen display set the limit. Obviously the drawings can not be displayed at their full resolution on the monitor's screen. The program processes each element stored in memory, and produces the screen display from this information. It has to work out a display that is as accurate as the screen resolution permits. The important point to note here, is that when a drawing is printed or plotted out, the program is not limited by the screen resolution. It again takes each element of the drawing, and produces it as accurately as possible on the hard copy. The accuracy with which the program stores the drawing is likely to be very much greater than the resolution of any current output device. Therefore, the quality of the hard copy is limited by the resolution of the printer or plotter, not by any constraints imposed by the program.

In theory you can produce drawings as complex as you like with a vector based graphics program, but in practice there will be some very definite limitations on what can be achieved. The first point to bear in mind is that the resolution of many output devices is not very high. A printer which operates at 120 dots per inch and prints out to a maximum size of 10 inches by 8 inches has a maximum resolution of 1200 × 960 dots. This is comparable to some high resolution monitors. If drawings take considerably less than the maximum printing area, then this effectively reduces the resolution of the printer. At 3 inches × 2 inches for instance, it would provide an effective resolution of 360 × 240 dots. This is comparable to low/medium resolution displays.

There are two points to note here. One is simply that the quality of the printout will not be very good at 120 d.p.i. For good quality graphics there is a lot to be said in favour of a resolution of 300 d.p.i. or more. The second point is that the amount of information that can be put into a drawing reproduced at this sort of resolution is strictly limited. There is no point in drawing up a complex piece of artwork which will just be a lot of incomprehensible lines and smudges when printed out. The larger the drawing can be printed, the more complex it can be made. Where a small drawing is needed it is usually better to print it out twice the required size and then have it photo-reduced. This gives a much better perceived quality, with (say) a 180 d.p.i. printer effectively operating as a 360 d.p.i. type.

Pan and Zoom

There is clearly a difficulty in getting complex drawings into the computer in the first place. Although the program can handle very high resolutions, the display can not. On the face of it, this prevents you from clearly seeing on the screen the drawing you are producing. In a way this is true, and I have produced numerous drawings which, when viewed in their entirely on the screen, really look like little more than random dots and lines! This limitation is overcome using the program's pan and zoom facilities. The zoom facility enables a small part of a drawing to be displayed across the whole screen so that even fine detail shows up clearly, and can be easily added to the drawing. The pan facility enables the part of the drawing that is being viewed to be altered. This is much the same as the pan and zoom facilities of many d.t.p. programs. However, these facilities are usually much more sophisticated on vector drawing programs. In most cases you can zoom-in on any desired area of the drawing, and can zoom-in on a very small area indeed if desired.

The pan and zoom facilities greatly enhance the capabilities of vector based drawing programs, enabling complex drawings that would otherwise be impractical to be produced with reasonable ease. Although it might seem that these facilities totally remove any limitations on the maximum size and complexity of drawings, things are not really quite as simple as this. The first problem is that panning and zooming takes a vast amount of complex calculations in order to convert the details of the drawing elements stored in memory into an appropriate screen display. This means that you can sit there watching the display for a considerable period of time before a new view is produced.

The time taken on pan and zoom operations depends on the complexity of the drawing, the operating speed of the computer, and how well or otherwise the program is written. Some systems can handle practically any pan or zoom operation in a second or two, while others take very much longer. In the early days of computer based drawing systems it was often a case of having a cup of tea while the "zoomed" screen was redrawn! Fortunately, most modern computer drawing systems are very much better than this. Even so, some complex drawings require so much panning and zooming that they become rather impractical to produce. A few vector drawing programs now offer multiple on-screen views of a drawing so that instead of repeatedly panning backwards and forwards between two zoomed views, you simply have them both on the screen at once, side-by-side or one above the other. It is generally only the more expensive programs that have this feature though.

It is best to be pragmatic about complex graphics. Rather than spend large amounts of time drawing up a complex illustration that can not be printed out in sufficient detail, it would be much better to split it into two drawings. These could be drawn up much more quickly and easily, and printed out in greater detail.

CAD or Illustration

As mentioned previously, vector graphics programs fall into two main categories. These are the CAD (computer aided drafting) and illustration programs. Although they may seem to be very similar superficially, they are very different to use, and are aimed at totally different users. There are a few programs which have facilities that put them somewhere between the two types of software, but even these programs tend to be heavily biased in one direction. Almost invariably they are basically illustration programs but with some CAD capabilities and features.

If we consider the CAD programs first, these are intended for the production of technical drawings, and are likely to be of little use for anything else. You can actually produce any type of drawing with good CAD programs, but they generally represent a relatively difficult (and possibly costly) method of producing business graphics, sketches, etc. The facilities offered by programs of this type are vast, and are far too numerous to be covered in detail here. There should be facilities for drawing straight lines of various thicknesses, circles, arcs, text in any size and at any angle, ellipses, polygons, and hatching enclosed areas. There should be on-screen rulers or grids plus a snap grid to make it easy to draw accurately to scale when necessary.

A good CAD program has excellent editing facilities. This is one respect in which a vector based program has a big advantage over a pixel based type. With a pixel based drawing program you can usually undertake editing such as copying or moving an area of screen to another part of the screen, but you can not pick out and edit individual drawing elements. If you select an area around (say) a circle, and move it to another position, you may take more than just the circle. If there was some text in the circle, then that will be moved along with the circle. If part of a line went through the circle, then this part of the line would be cut away from the rest of the line and moved!

Vector based drawing programs do not have this problem, since they have each drawing element stored in memory as a separate entity. You usually have the ability to pick out one element, or possibly a group of drawing elements, and to then move, copy, rotate, or rescale them. More basic editing commands permit individual end points of lines to be shifted, pieces of line to be trimmed away, and lines to be extended to meet other lines. The number of commands available with even the more simple CAD programs is quite large. In order to produce quite simple technical drawings you will need quite an array of commands at your disposal.

With some types of software that have large numbers of functions it is just a matter of finding and learning the ten or twenty percent of these functions that are actually of use to you. Word processors are a good example of this. It is generally reckoned that most users only actually utilize about fifteen percent of the available functions, and ignore about eighty-five percent of them! With drawing programs the reverse is probably true. You will probably need to use about eighty or ninety percent of the available functions. It will inevitably take a fair amount of time in order to get everything set up and operating properly, and to learn to use the program efficiently. If you are going to use one of these programs properly you need to be fairly technically minded. Practically anyone can "doodle" with paint software, but it is much more difficult to produce something sensible using a CAD program. Presumably though, if you need to produce technical drawings using a CAD program, you will have a suitable scientific or technical background.

When dealing with CAD programs you will encounter references to "layers", and most CAD software can handle large numbers of layers. Layers are often likened to drawing using a pen on transparent film. Rather than drawing the whole thing onto one piece of film, you can draw different parts of the drawing onto different pieces of film. If you place the pieces of film one on top of the other, you can see the complete drawing. If some aspects of the drawing are not required, the appropriate piece or pieces of film are removed.

In a computer context I suppose it is true to say that the layers are notional rather than real. Each drawing element in the computer's memory is tapped with its notional layer number. If you switch off a layer, any element in the drawing having that layer number is ignored, and not displayed. This gives an effect much like the layers of transparent film analogy, and the same degree of control. In fact there is a greater level of control, because it is normally possible to shift elements of the drawing from one layer to another if desired. In a colour system a different colour is normally used for each layer so that you can see which layer each drawing element is on. Perhaps of greater importance, it makes it immediately apparent if you should start drawing something on the wrong layer. Layers are essential to some specialist types of drawing (such as printed circuit design), and can be useful for general illustration work. It is probably best not to use them just for the sake of it though. You would probably just confuse matters rather than making life easier.

Another standard feature of CAD program is the ability to handle symbols. In this context symbols are pieces of predrawn artwork that can be called up from disk and added into drawings wherever you like, and as often as you like. In conventional drafting it is normal for stencils to be used where the same things must be drawn time and time again, in drawing after drawing. More recently rub-on transfers have been used for this type of thing. These both have the disadvantage of only being practical where something will have to be drawn a very large number of times. The cost of having custom stencils or rub-on transfers produced is normally too high unless something must be drawn up hundreds or even thousands of times.

The same is not true of CAD symbols where you can quickly draw up practically any desired symbol. There is no cost involved – only your time. Obviously symbols are not of use in all types of drawing, but for many types of technical drawing and illustration they can save massive amounts of time. Symbols are probably used most in diagrams, such as circuit diagrams (Figure 4.3). However, they can be of value in many types of technical illustration.

Some CAD programs are very expensive, and very sophisticated. These often have macro facilities. This enables repetitive tasks to be carried out largely automatically, which can save a lot of time (and tedium). Some programs go a stage further, and actually have programming languages which enable you to produce your own drawing commands. This type of thing can save vast amounts of time when undertaking many types of drawing. However, it takes a very long time to get the program customised and functioning just the way you want it.

Coupled with the cost of these up-market CAD programs, and the technical know-how needed to get everything working properly, they can only be recommended for those who undertake large amounts of technical drawing. For the occasional user one of the simpler CAD programs, specifically designed for non-regular users, is a much more practical proposition.

3D CAD

Some form of three dimensional capability is a feature of many medium priced and up-market CAD programs. The sophistication of the three dimensional

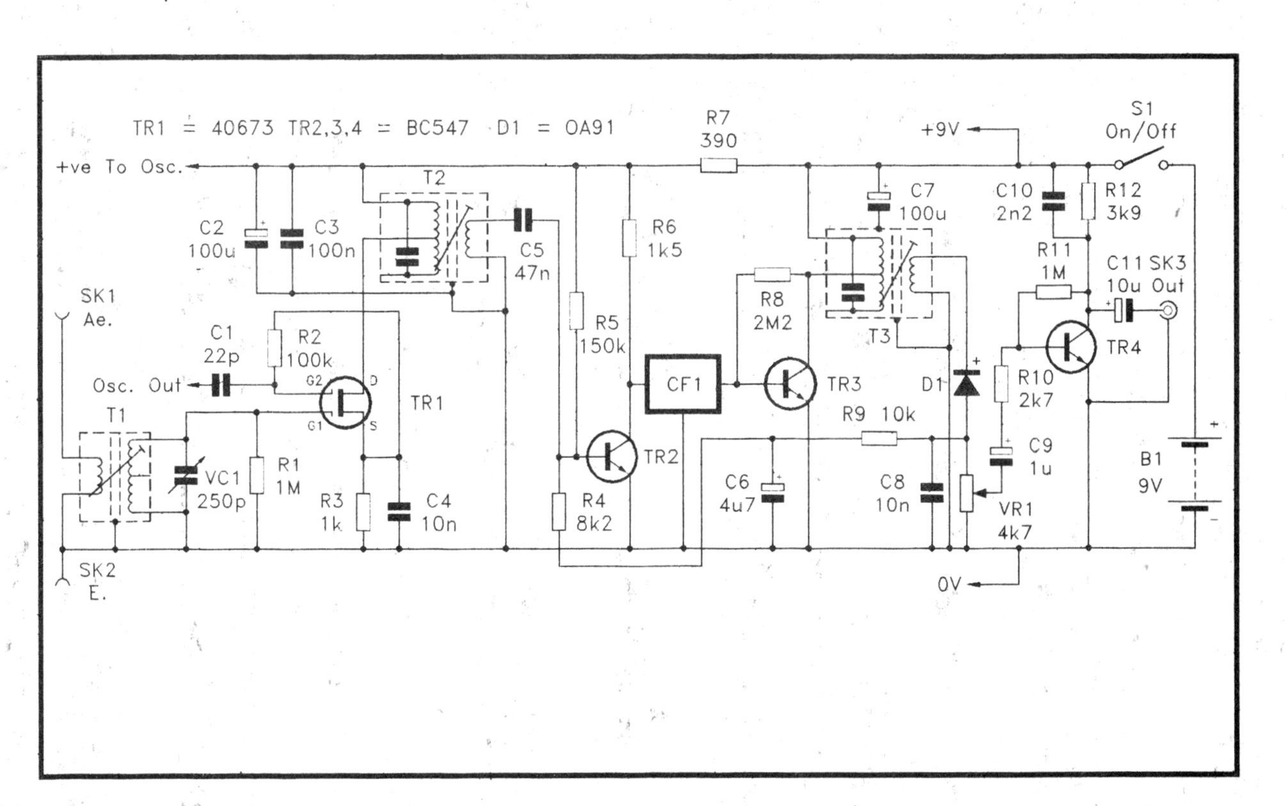

Fig. 4.3 Symbols are useful where the same drawing elements are used over and over again, as in this circuit diagram. Note how vector graphics easily cope with the complexity of this drawing

capabilities varies enormously, and in general you get what you pay for. Some have what are often termed two-and-a-half dimensional facilities. The drawings produced are three dimensional in that they are proper three dimensional views. In fact they are isometric views in most cases. This is a convenient but slightly non-scientific form of three dimensional view. The drawings are two dimensional in that there are only "X" and "Y" dimensions, with no true "Z" dimension being used. What this means in practice is that you draw up a three dimensional view, and that is the only view you get. If you need a view from a different side, you must start again.

With true three dimensional drawing programs you supply X, Y, and Z co-ordinates for each end of every line, arc, etc., in the drawing. It is then possible to view the drawing from any angle and distance. You are putting into the computer an accurate three dimensional model of the subject, and then generating as many different views as you need from this computerised model. A few programs, particularly those intended for architectural use, actually let you view the drawing from the inside! Apparently the idea is to draw up a room, complete with furnishings, and then let clients see what it looks like from the inside. Again, you can have several different views looking from different viewpoints and in different directions.

The more simple three dimensional CAD programs are of the so-called "wire frame" variety. In other words, the objects depicted in the drawing are simple "see through" frames and do not have any proper surfaces. Other programs have hidden line removal facilities that give the impression of solid surfaces. At the top end of the market there are true surface modelling programs which give shaded surfaces, and an extremely realistic effect. In some cases the CAD program does not have these shading facilities built-in, but can have the drawings it produces processed by a separate shading or "rendering" program.

Three dimensional CAD programs can produce some very impressive looking results, but this type of drawing is not something to be undertaken lightly. Most programs of this type are quite expensive, and many of them will only run properly on some quite sophisticated and costly hardware. Even with two dimensional drawing programs there tends to be a sort of mental block when you first use them. This is not really surprising, since after spending a lifetime drawing using pens, pencils, and paper, the switch to a mouse and a monitor screen is a large one. After some experience with a drawing program though, most people get used to the new way of doing things. Presumably, over a period of time the computer system becomes the normal way of drawing, while pencil and paper become quite alien!

With three dimensional drawing programs there is the additional problem of having to think in three dimensions while actually working on a two dimensional display. Even if you are used to using two dimensional CAD programs, this is still quite a leap for the mind. Three dimensional CAD programs provide help in making this leap, such as multiple views of the drawing, but it still requires a lot of effort and skill on the part of the draughtsman. This type of drawing is really a very specialised area of computer graphics, and one that the occasional user might never master.

Illustration Programs

As already pointed out, illustration programs are vector based drawing programs, like CAD software. On the other hand, to use they are often much more reminiscent of paint programs than CAD programs. This is something that depends on the particular program concerned, and an illustration program that is designed primarily for producing technical illustrations will have strong similarities to CAD programs. Most illustration programs are not primarily designed for this type of thing though, and they have the emphasis on freehand drawing facilities (like paint programs), rather than drawing to scale using straight lines, circles, etc. I would not wish to give the idea from this that there are no straight line and circle functions in illustration programs. They are generally equipped with a reasonable range of drawing tools. The drawing facilities of this type generally fall well short of CAD standards, but the freehand drawing facilities tend to be much superior.

On the face of it, paint programs are suitable for much illustration work. In reality they are often totally inadequate due to their relatively low resolution. On the screen and on the final printout, diagonal lines often have a pronounced staircase effect. Circles and arcs tend to look rather rough, and the general quality is inadequate where high quality hard copy is required. Some paint programs do actually have printer routines that to some extent smooth out the "rough edges" on the printouts, but usually these still fall well short of the quality required in demanding applications.

The obvious solution to the problem is to have a freehand drawing program that uses vector based graphics rather than pixel based graphics. This is fine in theory, but implementing a practical system is quite difficult. For drawing straight lines, circles, etc., it is possible to adopt an approach which is much like the one used in CAD programs. The drawing entities are stored in memory as objects of particular types, at certain co-ordinates, and of a certain size. They are then reproduced on the screen, printer, or whatever, at the maximum resolution of the device concerned.

The main problem is in achieving a method of freehand drawing that will give a very high quality output on suitable printers and plotters. It is easy enough to have a program that lets you draw on the screen in paint program fashion, but how is this relatively low resolution drawing then converted into high quality hard copy. As pointed out previously, there are routines that can give "smoothed" printed output from paint programs, but these routines are not totally successful. It would be unreasonable to expect a program to invent added resolution and to always get it right.

The usual solution adopted in illustration programs is to use Bezier curves. The best way to learn about Bezier curves is to experiment with a suitable illustration program for a few minutes. It soon becomes very obvious and easy to get the exact curve you require. I can explain the basic principle

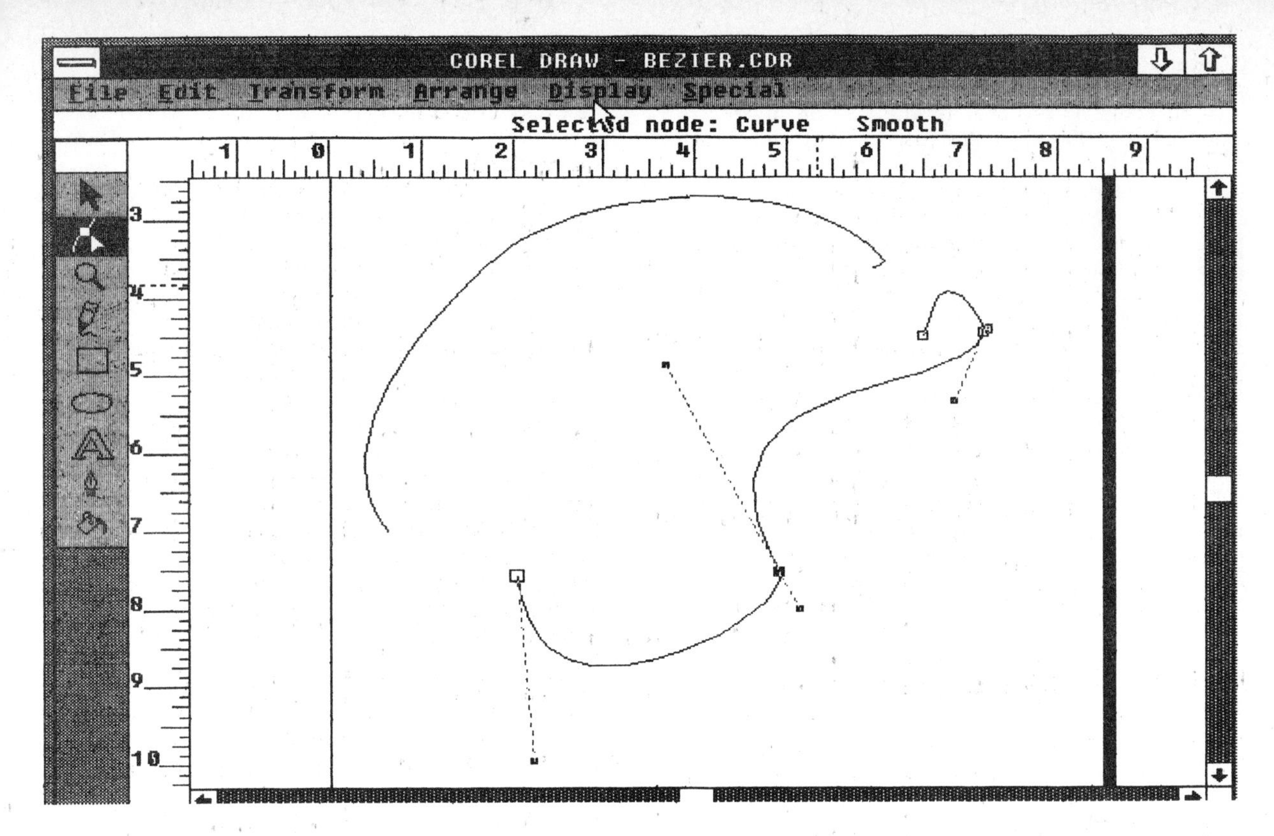

Fig. 4.4 Two Bezier curves produced using Corel Draw! The lower one is a multiple type, and some of the control points/lines are shown

here, but this may make it all seem a bit more cumbersome than it really is. A Bezier curve is controlled by two lines, one at each end of the curve. The angles of the lines set the start and finish directions of the curve. The lengths of the lines control the sharpness of the curve. A short line gives a sharp curve initially, followed by relatively straight line. A long line gives a long steady curve. The two lines each control about half of the curve, and together they give tremendous control over the curve, permitting complex shapes to be produced with just a single Bezier curve. Figure 4.4 shows some example Bezier curves, complete with their control lines. Of course, normally the control points and lines would optionally be shown on the screen for editing purposes, but would not appear on the hard copy.

Although one Bezier curve can be manipulated into some complex shapes, practical drawings often require such complex shapes that a single Bezier curve can not accommodate them. The solution to this problem is to have two or more Bezier curves joined end to end. This permits any curve to be accurately reproduced. With some programs you have to produce the Bezier curves by indicating the control points, which can then be dragged around the screen if the curve produced was not as expected.

Alternatively, some programs let you draw freehand on the screen, and the shape you have drawn is automatically converted into a Bezier curve or curves. It can take a while for complex shapes to be converted into corresponding Bezier curves, but I find this method much quicker and easier. Again, if things do not turn out quite as expected, you can simply pull the control points around the screen using the mouse and on-screen pointer, and soon get things pulled into shape.

There are alternatives to Bezier curves, mainly in the form of varieties of spline curve. With these you place a series of points on the screen, and the program then works out a curve that passes through these points. With certain types of spline curve the line does not necessarily pass through the intermediate points, it may simply pass close to them. With all the spline curve generators I have encountered, the line always touches the first and final points used.

Spline curves might seem like a better way of handling things, but in practice they are often awkward to use. In order to define a complex curve accurately it is often necessary to indicate a large number of points. In fact it can often be necessary to put down a large number of points in order to produce relatively simple shapes. This can make it relatively slow and difficult to indicate a rough initial shape, and more time consuming to edit it into precisely the required shape. The main problem is that spline curves generally tend to be a bit unpredictable.

The most predictable types are the ones that produce lines with a minimum of curvature, which pass through the points placed on the screen. These tend to give something not far removed from a series

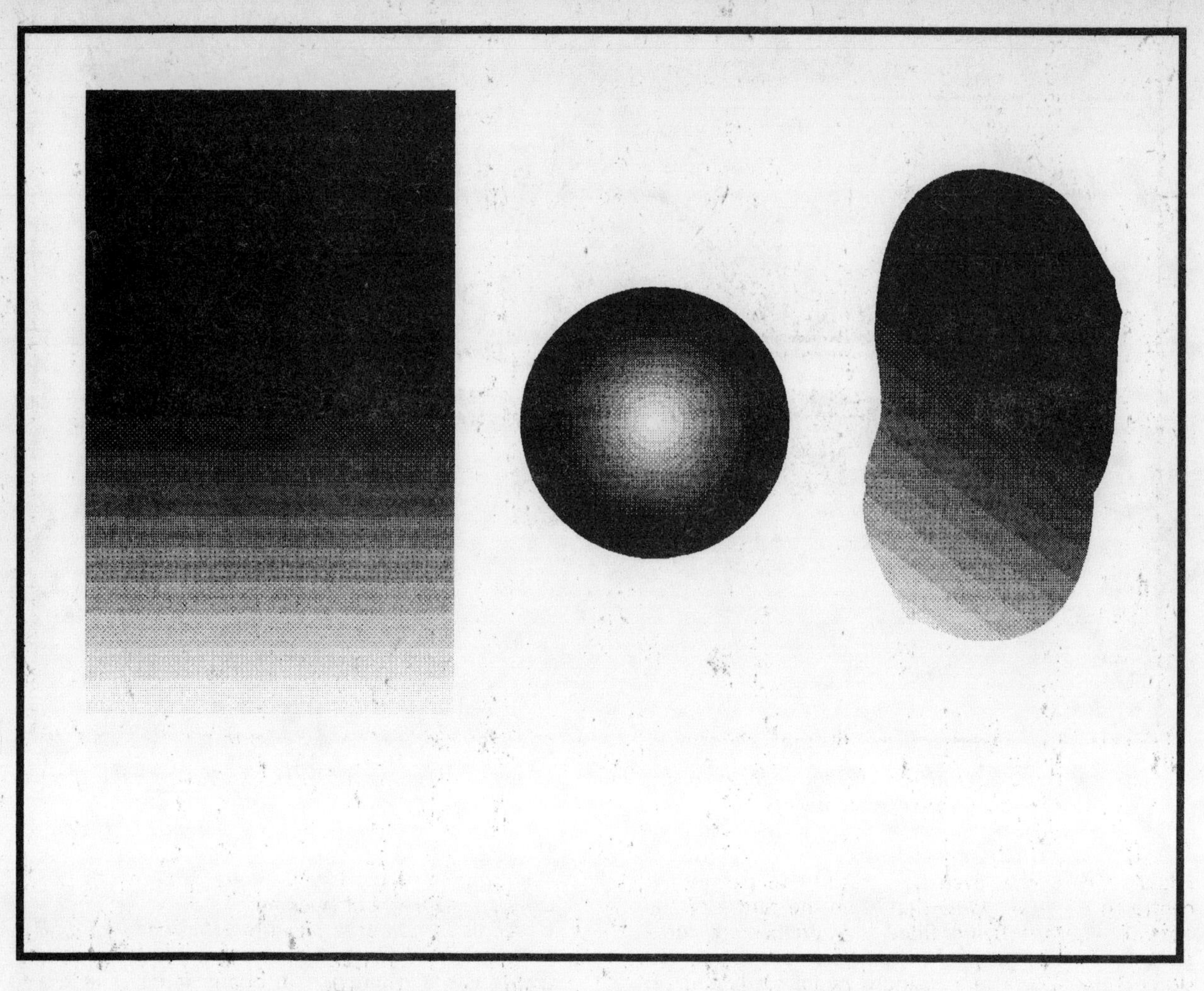

Fig. 4.5 Some examples of graduated (fountain) fills, including a radial type (centre)

of straight lines at angles to one another. For many types of drawing this gives unsatisfactory results. The spline curves that give smoother results generally give a much better final product, but are difficult to predict because the line does not usually pass through the intermediate points, and in some cases might not actually pass all that close to them.

Bezier curves enable complex shapes to be produced using a minimum number of control points, and once a basic shape has been produced it is possible to quickly and easily "fine tune" it. Things are especially easy with the programs which enable you to draw onto the screen, and which then work out suitable Bezier curves for you. Matters are far less straightforward if you have to work out the positions of the control points for yourself. However, with practice most users soon learn to work efficiently using this method.

Fills

A common and important feature of illustration programs is some form of "fill" facility. At its most basic level this just consists of a command that enables an indicated area of the drawing to be filled in with the desired colour (or shade of grey if you are working in monochrome). Most fill facilities go well beyond this basic level though. Often it is possible to fill areas with complex patterns. This is a feature of many paint programs incidentally, and I suppose that the hatching feature of many CAD programs is comparable to this.

Perhaps the most useful type of fill is the graduated type, or a "fountain" fill as it is sometimes called. With these the colour of the fill varies from the specified start colour to the specified finishing colour. In a black and white system the graduation is between two selected shades of grey (or from black right through to white). A typical application of a fountain fill would be to produce a background that went from (say) light yellow at the top, through orange to deep red at the bottom. This type of thing tends to give more lively and pleasing results than a background of a single colour.

Most programs that have this feature enable the direction of the graduation to be specified. In other words, the colour change does not have to be from top to bottom; it can be from side to side or diagonally at any desired angle. In most cases there is also a radial graduation option. This has the start colour at the centre, and the finishing colour around the

Fig. 4.6 A simple 3D effect. All four cars are drawn in their entirety. The program removes lines and fills that are obscured by foreground objects

edges. There may even be a facility to permit the centre to be offset somewhat from the centre of the drawing element being filled. A typical use for a graduated radial fill is to give a circle a three dimensional look. In effect, using a radial graduated fill on a circle converts it into a sphere. Figure 4.5 shows some example graduated fills.

Illustration programs do not usually provide much help in producing three dimensional views. It is assumed that the user will have sufficient artistic ability to handle the perspective, etc., properly. There are often a few aids though, and probably the most useful of these is the ability to stack up objects one in front of the other. As a simple example, suppose that you draw up a front view of a car. You could then make a slightly smaller copy of this, and offset it slightly to one side. Most illustration programs permit groups of drawing objects to be selected and rescaled in this way. You could repeat this operation a few times, producing a series of car drawings of diminishing size, and increasingly offset from the original.

As it stands, all this gives you is a confusing mass of overlapping and intermingled car drawings that would probably not look like anything much at all. However, if the car drawings are stacked in sequence, with the largest at the front and the smallest at the rear, you get what looks like a line of cars tailing off into the distance. The program provides all the necessary hidden line and shading removal, so that objects towards the rear do not show through those towards the front. There may be a limit on the number of objects that can be stacked in this way, but normally this limit is quite large. Figure 4.6 shows an example of stacking.

Another powerful feature of most illustration programs is their text handling capabilities. Apart from having numerous different fonts available in practically any desired size, there are usually facilites to permit clever things to be done with the text strings, or possibly with individual characters in each piece of text. Just what can be achieved varies considerably from one illustration program to another, but these are some typical facilities. Fills and graduated fills can be used on text strings or applied to characters separately. In other words you could have a text string graduated from (say) yellow on the first letter, through green in the middle, ending up with blue on the last letter. Alternatively, each individual character could have this yellow to blue graduation.

Further facilities permit the shapes of characters to be altered. One way in which this can operate is to have the text characters, in effect, as normal graphics shapes with control points. By moving the control points you can alter the shape of any text character in any desired fashion. It is also possible to shift individual characters, either for manual kerning purposes, or for special effect. Individual control of the size of characters can be used to provide some interesting effects. The letters could be small initially, gradually getting larger towards the end of the text string. An advanced feature of some illustration program permits text to be wrapped around a graphics object, or perhaps even around a large text character.

For technical drawings and some other applications this type of thing is obviously not of great use. For advertising and many general illustration purposes it is very useful though, and permits an imaginative designer to produce some stunning results relatively quickly and easily. For some types of single page document an illustration program is all you need. You can produce and print out the finished pages from the illustration program, with no need to load them into a d.t.p. program for final processing prior to printing out.

A really good illustration program is probably the best type of drawing program for general illustration work. They can handle just about any drawing task (within reason), and can produce very high quality results. There are a few drawbacks, one of which is that this type of software is very demanding on the hardware. Powerful illustration programs require fast 16-bit computers with good displays. Until recently there were few programs of this type to choose from, even if you had a suitably powerful computer. This situation has changed in recent times, and for some computers there is now a reasonable range of illustration software from which you can select the program that best suits your needs. Illustration software is not as difficult and time consuming to learn to use as CAD software, but it is far less straightforward to use than paint programs. You can usually learn to produce some simple illustrations in a fairly short time, but it might take quite a while before the program is fully mastered. If you will be doing a reasonable amount of illustration work, it is likely to be well worth the effort required in order to learn every aspect of such a program.

Importing Graphics

The easiest way to add graphics into a d.t.p. produced document is to simply reserve areas on the pages using the d.t.p. program, and to then print out the documents without the graphics.. Next use the graphics program to print out the illustrations at the correct sizes, and paste them in place. This is a rather old fashioned way of handling things, but remember that it may not always be possible to load your illustrations into the d.t.p. program. Some d.t.p. programs are more accommodating than others in this respect. In general, programs that produce pixel type graphics are better supported than those that produce vector graphics.

It is important to realise that even if graphics can be imported into a d.t.p. program, which might require an indirect route, they might undergo unacceptable changes in the process. Exchanging graphics between programs is far more complex than text interchanges, particularly where vector graphics are involved. The paste-up method may be crude and old fashioned, but it can be applied using practically any d.t.p. and graphics software combination, and should ensure that very high quality results are obtained.

If you are lucky, your d.t.p. program will be able to directly import drawing files produced by your graphics program. Your chances of being able to do this are much better if the graphics program is a very popular type, or is one which can produce files that are in the same format as a popular graphics program. Assuming that the graphics program can produce drawings in a suitable file format, there should be no difficulty in loading the drawings into d.t.p. documents.

In some cases you might have the luxury of being able to produce drawing files in two or more formats that the d.t.p. program can read. If this should be the case it is probably worthwhile trying to load some typical illustrations in each of these formats. One format might be quicker and easier to use than the others, or it might give more faithful transfer of the drawings. With pixel based graphics it might not make any difference which format is used. With vector graphics there can be vast differences in the results obtained using different formats. In general, using a format that converts the vector graphics to a screen pixel format (such as an AutoCAD "slide" file) will give lower quality than one which transfers the drawing in vector graphics form. On the other hand, if the pixel format gives adequate results, this might be the quickest and most reliable method.

When transferring drawings in vector graphic form there are several potential problem areas. One of them is the text. If you have a drawing which has something like boxes containing nicely centred pieces of text, you might find that after the transfer the text is no longer centred properly. This type of thing seems to occur due to slight changes in the text size. In some cases the text grows so large that it goes well outside its normal limits, giving totally unusable results.

Another common problem area is line widths. These days most vector graphics programs are not restricted to a single line width. In fact most CAD and illustration programs permit you to use any line width you like. You may find that some file formats result in line width information being lost. This does not necessarily result in drawings being rendered totally useless after the transfer to the d.t.p. program, but there will clearly be an appreciable loss of quality. You may find that the single line width used gives lines that are too fat, or that line width information is to some extent retained, but all the lines seem too wide. This type of thing can sometimes be corrected by altering the scaling or line widths in the drawing program. For example, halving all the line widths may give better results, as might drawing everything double size but leaving the line widths unaltered. If things do not go right first time, some experimentation will often result in more acceptable results.

Aspect Ratio

A problem that can be very difficult (or impossible) to cure is that of aspect ratios. Preserving the aspect ratio of graphics is not always important. Indeed, many d.t.p. programs have the ability to alter the aspect ratio of imported graphics so that they can be placed in a frame of any desired size. With some diagrams and other illustrations, particularly those that contain circles, even quite minor distortions of the aspect ratio can be very noticeable. With programs that can vary the aspect ratio of graphics there may be no real problem, since you can use this feature to correct the aspect ratio, by trial and error if necessary. Note though, that this feature might only be applicable to pixel based graphics, and might not work on any imported vector graphics.

If the d.t.p. program can not cure the problem, it might be possible to cure it at the drawing stage. Some drawing programs have an aspect ratio control, but this usually only affects the way the drawings are displayed on screen. This type of control does not always have any effect on the stored drawing files. On the other hand, if you are using some form of screen "grabber" to save screens to a file, an aspect ratio control of this type might correct matters. It might also be effective with pixel based drawing programs. There is always the possibility of drawing the illustrations with a deliberately distorted aspect ratio, so that the distortion produced when importing them into the d.t.p. program gives the correct aspect ratio overall. This sounds easy enough, but is likely to prove very difficult to achieve in practice.

Sometimes a cure can be effected if the root cause can be found. With vector graphics the problem is most likely to be caused by a "bug" in one of the routines that handles the transfer of the graphics files. There is little that you can do about this other than point out the problem to the software companies involved, and hope that the problem is soon corrected. With pixel graphics the problem is often due to different screen resolutions being used for the drawing program and the d.t.p. program. Most computers can operate at several graphics screen resolutions, and these are some typical ones for IBM PCs and compatibles.

Graphics Adaptor	*Screen Resolution(s)*
CGA	320 x 200 and 640 x 200
Hercules	720 x 348
EGA	640 x 200 and 640 x 350
VGA	320 x 200 and 640 x 480
Super VGA	800 x 600

The point to note here is that while the ratio of the horizontal resolution to the vertical resolution varies considerably from one standard to another, the monitors always have (more or less) a 5 to 4 aspect ratio. Although one might expect the pixels to be square, it is clear from these figures that this is not the case. Some screen resolutions have pixels that are a little wider than they are high, while others have pixels that are very much taller than they are wide.

The practical importance of this is that aspect ratio problems can arise if the d.t.p. program operates on the basis of loading programs on a simple one-to-one pixel basis. If the drawing was produced using a different screen resolution to the one used for the d.t.p. program, this will clearly give some distortion of the graphics. With some screen combinations the problem could be quite severe. With a drawing done in the 640 x 200 CGA mode for example, it could appear severely "squashed" if loaded into a program running in the 640 x 480 VGA mode. Ideally the d.t.p. program should automatically compensate for the differences in the pixel ratios of different graphics screens, but not all actually do so. It might be necessary to make sure that the drawing and d.t.p. programs run in the same modes in order to avoid these problems.

Conversions

Ideally, when swapping graphics between a drawing program and a d.t.p. type it would be possible to do so by loading ordinary drawing files direct into the drawing program. Unfortunately, it is often not possible to import drawing files in their native format. Many drawing programs now have the ability to produce drawing files in several different formats. Also, most d.t.p. programs that can import graphics can handle several formats. This gives a good chance of being able to save drawings in a format that can be directly loaded into the d.t.p. program.

Where this is not possible, it might still be possible to achieve a successful file transfer by using a graphics conversion program. Some drawing and d.t.p. programs are supplied with one or more utilities of this type. They are also available as commercial programs and as shareware for some computers. It might even be necessary to convert from one file format to another, then to a third, and then finally import the illustration into the d.t.p. program. This might be a little time consuming, but it might get the job done satisfactorily.

In general it is better to avoid conversion programs completely, if at all possible. The problems that can arise when swapping graphics between a drawing program and a d.t.p. program have already be mentioned. The more processes that the drawings go through, the greater the chances of problems arising. With pixel based graphics the most likely problems are ones caused by different screen formats. Potential problems with changes in the aspect ratios of drawings have already been mentioned. With conversion programs there are other potential difficulties with screen formats.

One of these is simply that the program might insist on particular input and output screen formats, and refuse to work if the input file uses the wrong format. Conversion programs that can work with a variety of input and output formats will not necessarily process the input file to make allowances for any differences between the input and output screen formats. There might just be a one-to-one translation regardless of the input and output resolutions. With the input resolution lower than the output resolution you might find that a drawing only occupies a fraction of its allotted space, usually up in one corner of the frame. If the input resolution is higher than the output resolution, a large part of the drawing will be clipped off.

With some computers (such as the Commodore Amigas) there is good compatibility between graphics packages, and problems in swapping pixel graphics are few and far between. With other computers (such as the IBM PCs and compatibles) there are numerous graphics standards and graphics file formats. This gives much more scope for problems to occur. If you wish to import graphics into a d.t.p. program it would be prudent to check the compatibility between the d.t.p. and graphics programs before buying either of them. Ideally you should actually try them out together to make sure there are no unforeseen problems when transferring illustrations from one to the other.

Vector Conversions

Translation of pixel graphics from one file format to another, provided problems with different screen resolutions can be avoided, are generally quite successful. It mainly involves quite simple and straightforward processing. If problems should occur, it may well be possible to sort them out using the d.t.p. program. I suppose that in theory, converting vector graphics from one format to another is a reasonably straightforward task. In practice vector graphics are generally more awkward.

The usual problem is that of one drawing program having object types and facilities that are absent from, or implemented in a very different fashion on another drawing program. This makes conversion in either direction problematic. Sometimes even quite fundamental information seems to be lost, such as layer, colour, and line width information. Sometimes this will not matter too much, or at all. This depends on the types of illustration involved.

A more serious problem is that of drawing objects disappearing from the converted drawing. This may simply be due to the drawing being too complex for the conversion program to handle. It can also occur because the d.t.p. program can not handle really complex vector graphics. It is more likely to occur because the input file contains objects that can not be easily translated into corresponding objects in the output file. The most common causes of problems are complex hatching patterns, lines that vary in width, and complex ellipses/arcs. Problems when importing text in vector graphics drawing have already been mentioned. Putting drawings through a graphics conversion program increases the chances of these problems.

Some change in the appearance of the text is only to be expected. This is simply because conversion programs often ignore the font used in the input file, and there may be no corresponding font in the output file format anyway. If a fancy font is used in the drawings, it may well be converted to a simple font (possibly even a very basic straight line type). This may not matter too much, but it can result in some high quality illustrations ending up with a rather scrappy appearance.

A problem I have encountered on one or two occasions is that of random lines appearing in the converted drawings. This is presumably due to bugs in some vector graphics conversion utilities. Unless you can get the software company to provide a properly debugged format conversion program, there is probably nothing that can be done about this. It might be possible to edit the drawings in the d.t.p. program, and delete the offending lines, but most d.t.p. software does not provide this sort of facility.

HPGL

In our experience the best vector graphics format to use when swapping drawings between two CAD programs, or a CAD program and a d.t.p. type, is the HPGL format. This is the language used to drive Hewlett Packard plotters, and HPGL simply stands for "Hewlett Packard Graphics Language". These plotters were very popular in the early days of computing, and as a result of this many plotter manufacturers have made their plotters HPGL compatible. This has led to virtually every vector graphics program having the ability to drive an HPGL plotter. The ability to output HPGL disk files is now a fairly standard feature, and some d.t.p. programs can read in these files.

The advantage of an HPGL file is that it results in no loss of information. The graphics program will have an HPGL driver which ensures that every object in the drawing is plotted out correctly, even if it is a very complex shape that has to be plotted as numerous very short lines. Even colour and layer information can be retained, since the HPGL format allows several different pens to be used. Different layers or colours can therefore be represented by different pens. As the HPGL format is not in any way tied to a particular type of computer, it is quite possible to swap these files between programs running on different computers.

The only problem here is in finding a way of getting the two computers to "talk" to each other. This can usually be achieved via their RS232C serial interfaces with the aid of a suitable cable and some simple file exchange software. In some cases a floppy disk from one computer can be read into a different computer, but in most cases this approach is not possible. Incidentally, there are some conversion programs that can handle the file formats of programs which run on a different make of computer (e.g. permit Amiga drawings to be converted into a common PC format), but this is relatively rare.

Although the HPGL solution is in many ways an ideal one for swapping vector graphics, it does have a couple of minor drawbacks. One is that of pen widths. When plotting out drawings it is quite normal to use pens of various widths. Any program reading in an HPGL file will have no way of knowing what line width each pen should have. Even if only one pen is used, the program reading in the file might default to an incorrect width, or simply draw everything with the minimum line width. Ideally it should be possible to specify a line width for each pen, but this facility is usually absent. This problem can usually be overcome by using the drawing program's line width control to produce thick lines, rather than using notional thick pens. With a little experimentation it is usually possible to produce good results.

The second problem is simply that HPGL files can be quite large. Some programs produce more compact files than others. The HPGL includes commands to handle such things as arcs, circles, and text of various sizes, but many CAD programs produce everything using simple line plotting commands. This is to ensure that everything is plotted out exactly as it should be, with no changes in text size, text font, etc. With a large circle perhaps being plotted as a few hundred very short straight lines, obviously some very large files can be generated.

There should be no problem when using a computer that has reasonably high capacity disk drives and plenty of memory, but I suppose that the potential to overload the system is always there. The only certain way of discovering what you can and can not get away with is to try transferring some fairly complex drawings to see how the system copes with them. In some cases quite complex graphics can be accommodated, but it will take a long time for the files to be generated, and for them to be read into the d.t.p. program.

PostScript

PostScript is something that tends to be associated with the more up-market laser printers, and it is a page description language. It has similarities with the HPGL in that it can accommodate simple graphics shapes, etc., but it goes well beyond this. It can handle text in numerous fonts and sizes, complex fill patterns, and just about anything you would ever need to print out. PostScript is independent of the resolution of any particular device, and it will always make full use of the available resolution. Although in the past it has been mainly used as a means of sending page descriptions from d.t.p. or graphics programs to high quality printers, it actually has much wider applications. It can be used to exchange text and (or) graphics between two computer based devices, or between programs running on the same system.

The ability to produce PostScript files is now an increasingly common feature of graphics programs, especially those that can produce high resolution graphics, but it is still far from being a universal feature. Some d.t.p. programs have the ability to read-in PostScript files, but this is again a feature that is far from universal. We can not claim to have had much practical experience of this type of file exchange, and can not really comment on how well or otherwise it works in practice. Like the swapping of HPGL files, it seems to involve quite large files in many cases, which could cause problems. However, where everything in the system can handle this method of graphics interchange, it would seem to offer an excellent method of handling things. It should give a very faithful transfer of any illustration, with nothing being left out or lost in the transfer, and no loss of quality.

Chapter 5
SCANNER GRAPHICS

When a d.t.p. document is to include illustrations, there are several ways in which they can be included. If the finished document is to be professionally printed, the original illustrations can be sent to the printer and included in the document by conventional means, as line or half-tone blocks. Alternatively, the illustrations can be prepared in electronic form, for example by a CAD or paint program, and included in the d.t.p. document. Where illustrations already exist on paper, it is possible for them to be converted into electronic digital form.

Even when illustrations are to be added by the printer, it may be helpful to include them in the d.t.p. document, to indicate position, and to help design the layout on the screen. When this is done, the illustrations should have "for position only" clearly marked over them.

A scanner is the standard method of converting a graphic in paper form into digital information which can be included in a d.t.p. document. The paper graphic can be a line drawing, a photograph, or any artwork of suitable size which is physically able to be scanned. That last part mostly means that the artwork should be flat, and, for some types of scanner, have a stable surface which will not be disrupted or smudged by the scanning operation. Pastel and charcoal drawings, for example, are not suitable for most types of scanner, unless they have been treated with a fixative. Some types of scanner can only be used with suitably thin, flexible originals.

Photographs for scanning must be in the form of prints. Scanners which can scan transparencies are very expensive items and fall well outside the range of what can be considered as d.t.p. equipment. Generally, both colour and black-and-white prints can be scanned, but the sensing elements in scanners (charge-coupled devices, or "CCDs"), whilst panchromatic, have a considerable bias in their sensitivity towards the red end of the spectrum. This can mean that flesh tones in a colour print can reproduce as too light a tone in a scan, and lips can tend to disappear. To overcome this problem, some scanners use a light source which is filtered to a yellow-green colour.

There are scanners which can scan a colour print and produce an output file with colour information, though as yet they are rare, and also expensive. (At the time of writing, the first colour hand scanners have just appeared, at prices approaching £400 including VAT.) At present, there are relatively few d.t.p. programs which can handle colour bit-mapped images of this sort. Most would convert them to black-and-white. However, it is obvious that the ability to reproduce this type of colour illustration is going to be an important part of the future for d.t.p.

Prints should be on a glossy or smooth semi-matt paper. Prints on a dead-matt surface may show very poor shadow gradation, which is to say that the dark mid-tones and blacks will run together, but this does not matter with some subjects. If a print is on a paper with a regular-textured surface (usually described as "silk"), this texture may be reproduced in the scan, either directly or as an interference pattern with the dot-pitch of the scanner. If only a textured print is available, and patterning is a problem, it is always worth trying different dot-pitches on the scanner to see if one gives a better result than the others (not all scanners have a choice of dot-pitch).

Prints need to be of good, but not excessive, contrast. Some scanners do have a contrast control, but using this to try to correct a poor quality original will hardly ever result in a really good quality scan. You can not add tones which are not present in a print by turning the scanner contrast down. A good deal of detail is always lost when scanning photographs, so subjects which rely on a lot of fine detail for their appeal are best avoided. Gradation is also lost, but despite this portraits, where gradation is normally considered very important, can scan very well.

With line drawings, if it is desired to reproduce the drawing as solid lines on a clean background, it is important that the density and thickness of the lines is consistent. Scanners almost invariably have a line setting for scanning this type of material, and this is basically a very high contrast setting. This makes the setting of the light-dark control (which again virtually all scanners have) critical. If the lines vary in thickness and blackness, and the density control is set light enough to give a clean background, the finer and lighter lines can be lost. On the other hand, if the density is turned up to ensure all the lines are copied, you are likely to get black spots, mottle, or patches in what should be a clean white background. In general, ink drawings are easier to scan than pencil drawings.

If variation of line is vital to the quality of a drawing, it can be reproduced as a grey-scale image. However, this will result in some loss of fine detail, as with photographs, and the background is unlikely to be reproducible as a completely clean white.

If it is desired to have half-tones in a drawing, you can either use a dot-pattern product like LetraTone in conjunction with the line-scan mode, or shading in conjunction with a grey-scale mode. If you try to combine dot-screens with grey-scale scanning, this is again likely to give problems with interference patterns. This will also be a problem if you try to scan a photograph which has been reproduced by dot-screening, and of course you are also likely to be infringing copyright.

Types of Scanner

There are three basic types of scanner: flat-bed, sheet-feed and hand-held, the last type often being called "handy scanners".

Flat-bed scanners are the most generally useful type for scanning photographs and all types of artwork. The original is laid face-down on a sheet of glass or clear plastic, and the scanner mechanism passes below this sheet during the actual scanning.

This type of scanner can handle virtually all types of flat original, as it does not involve any frictional contact with the surface, and does not bend or otherwise stress the material. It can also easily handle originals which are smaller than the maximum size the scanner can take. The majority of flat-bed scanners take originals up to A4 size, but larger versions are available. Flat-bed scanners are usually the most expensive type, size-for-size.

Sheet-fed scanners pass the original being scanned past the scanner head using a system of rollers similar to the paper feed in a printer. This inevitably involves a certain amount of rubbing of the surface and flexing of the material, and so is unsuitable for scanning some types of artwork. Scanners of this type can also have problems with photographic prints on very glossy or very thick paper, which may skid on the rollers, or be too inflexible for the mechanism, respectively. The smallest size of original which can be scanned may not be much less than the maximum size. If you want to scan a small photograph, for instance, it may be necessary to tape it to a larger "carrier" sheet (with some risk of it jamming in the mechanism). Scanners of this type are primarily designed for use with optical character recognition software for reading in pages of printed text. They are a little less expensive than flat-bed scanners.

Hand scanners are the smallest and least expensive of scanners. The original to be scanned is laid on a suitable flat surface, and the scanner is rolled over it by hand. The first scanners of this type could scan a width of 65mm, or about 2¼ inches, which frankly is too small to be of much use. Current versions can scan 105mm, or 4 inches, which is much more workable, being wide enough for most columns of text, and ideal for enprint-size photographs. Larger versions with a scanning width of over 8 inches (suitable for scanning a full A4 sheet), have been made, but have not achieved much commercial success. The results turned in by these small scanners can be surprisingly good, for all types of original. The scanning does involve a degree of physical skill, to keep the scanner straight and the movement smooth, but this is not too difficult to learn. This type of scanner is quite inexpensive, and available for computers such as the Apple Macintosh, Atari ST, Amiga and Acorn Archimedes, as well as for the IBM PC and compatibles. Figure 5.1 shows a typical hand scanner.

One unusual type of scanner worth mentioning is a flat-bed type made by the Japanese company Chinon. The original to be scanned is placed face up on a baseboard, and the scanner system is like a camera, supported on a column and looking straight down on the original. This type of scanner is ideal for any artwork with a loose surface, and can also scan three-dimensional objects, provided the relief is not too great. Two models are made, giving pitches of either 200 d.p.i. or 300 d.p.i. No light source is included.

Grey Scales and Dithering

When an original having a range of half-tones (that is, shades of grey between black and white), is scanned, some means must be used to represent those grey tones within the file generated by the scanner. There are two ways of doing this.

It is possible to assign a density value to every point scanned. If, for example, each point scanned is given one byte in the file, it can have one of 256 values assigned to it. In fact, only a very few flat-bed scanners are capable of generating true grey scale information, and they tend to be the more expensive. (A more moderately priced sheet-fed scanner with this capability has recently been introduced.)

When a file containing true grey-scale information is imported into a d.t.p. program, the program can make contrast and density changes to the image, making it possible to fine-tune it for the printer in use. However, not all d.t.p. programs can do this. Again, it is usually found only in the more expensive packages, like Xerox Ventura Publisher and Aldus Pagemaker.

A disadvantage of the true grey-scale system is that it tends to result in very large files, especially if a large original is scanned at a high resolution. There are, as yet, no true grey-scale printers. This means that when the image is printed, the half-tones have to be produced by varying the spacing of the printer dots. In the dark parts of the picture, most of the possible dots are printed, whereas in the lighter parts fewer are printed. This process is known as dithering.

In order to produce smaller image files, the dithering can be done at an earlier stage, either in the scanner software, or in the scanner itself. When this is done, each point in the scan is either printed or not printed, so can be represented by a single bit in the file. However, when a scan is generated in dithered form, it cannot subsequently be altered easily, either in density or contrast. Most scanners can produce dithered images directly. In the case of flat-bed scanners with true grey-scale capability, the dithering may be done by the scanner itself, or subsequently in software. With hand and sheet-fed scanners, it is normally done within the scanner.

The best of current hand-scanners offer a choice of three sets of dither patterns. These differ in the coarseness of the screening effect they produce. The finest setting is the one which should be used to get the best results for printing on computer printers. The other settings produce a dot-screened type of image, and are used when the printing is to be done with a proper phototypesetting machine with a resolution of 1200 d.p.i. upwards. The quality of the paper determines which setting should be used.

The coarser settings are also useful if a scanned picture is to be printed out on a high-resolution printer, and then subsequently distributed as photocopies. When this is done, the finest setting may "block up", making the picture reproduce as a grey rectangle. The coarser settings are much less likely to block up in this way. They can also be used for graphic effect. Figure 5.2 shows the line/dither setting control on a hand scanner. Figures 5.3 to 5.5 show the results of using the three dither settings on this scanner, Figure 5.3 being the optimum dither setting, Figure 5.4 the fine dot-screen, and Figure 5.5 the coarse dot-screen. The photograph was scanned at 200 d.p.i., and the printer used was an H-P PaintJet, with 180 d.p.i. resolution.

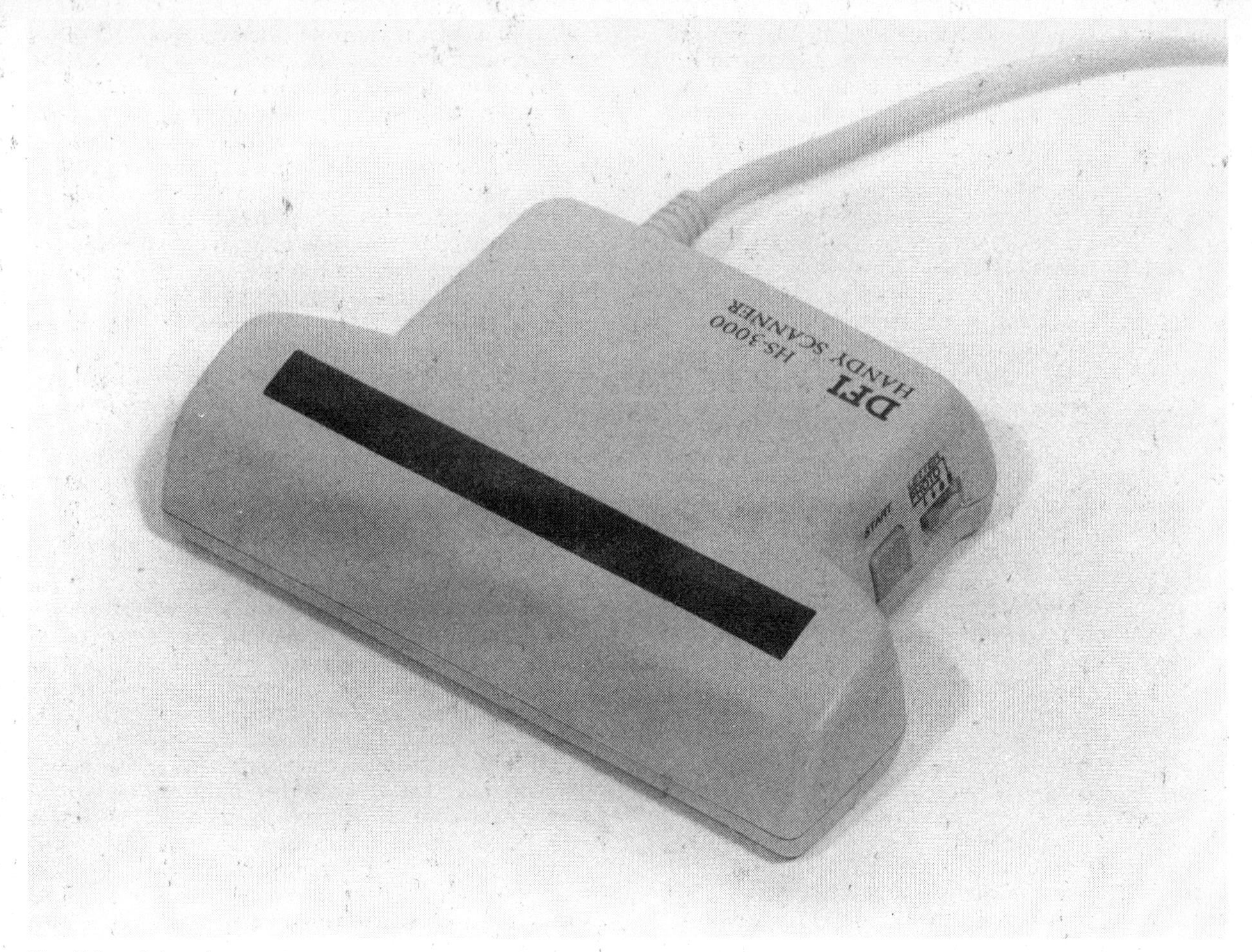

Fig. 5.1   A hand scanner

The quality of gradation in the image depends on the number of steps allowed between white and black. The higher the number of steps, the better the gradation. In the case of true grey-scale information, increasing the number of steps will increase the size of the file. To allow 256 steps needs 8 bits for each point in the picture, to allow 16 steps needs 4. In the case of dithered image files, there is a trade-off between the number of steps and the detail which can be retained.

Dithering is performed by dividing the picture into cells. The larger these cells, the better the gradation which can be produced. If each cell is 4 × 4 pixels, there are 17 possible gradations, from printing none of the dots to printing all 16. For a 6 × 6 pixel square, there are 37 possible gradations, and for an 8 × 8 square, 65. (In practice, cells of this size are used for 16, 32 and 64 steps respectively as this fits in better with binary arithmetic.) The dither patterns within these cells are carefully designed to give the best "scatter" of pixels in the cell, avoiding obvious patterning.

On the face of it, if you are scanning at 300 d.p.i. and using a 6 × 6 dither pattern, this should reduce the possible resolution to 50 d.p.i. In fact, it is not as simple as this as, especially when the dithering is done directly in the scanner, it is possible for a cell to be made up partly of one pattern, partly of another. This means that a dark line can pass through a light cell, so retention of high-contrast detail can be better than might be thought. However, the cell size does have an effect on the detail, and especially on low contrast detail.

When the number of steps of gradation is low, the effect known as "contouring" will be apparent. With 16 steps, contouring will be quite obvious on any subject with continuous tones. With 32 steps, contouring will still occur, but only becomes really obvious on subjects like portraits. With 64 steps, you will generally only see the contouring if you look for it. Thirty-two steps can be considered acceptable for the majority of d.t.p. applications. Unfortunately, most flat-bed and sheet-fed scanners only offer 16-step dithering. Many hand-scanners actually do better, with 32 steps. In technical descriptions of scanners, you will sometimes see the terms 16-bit or 32-bit used to describe the number of steps of gradation.

Dot-Pitches, Sizing and Scaling

The dot-pitch of a scanner is the distance between the points on the original at which the scanner takes a reading. It is normally expressed in dots per inch, and may be regarded as a measure of how much

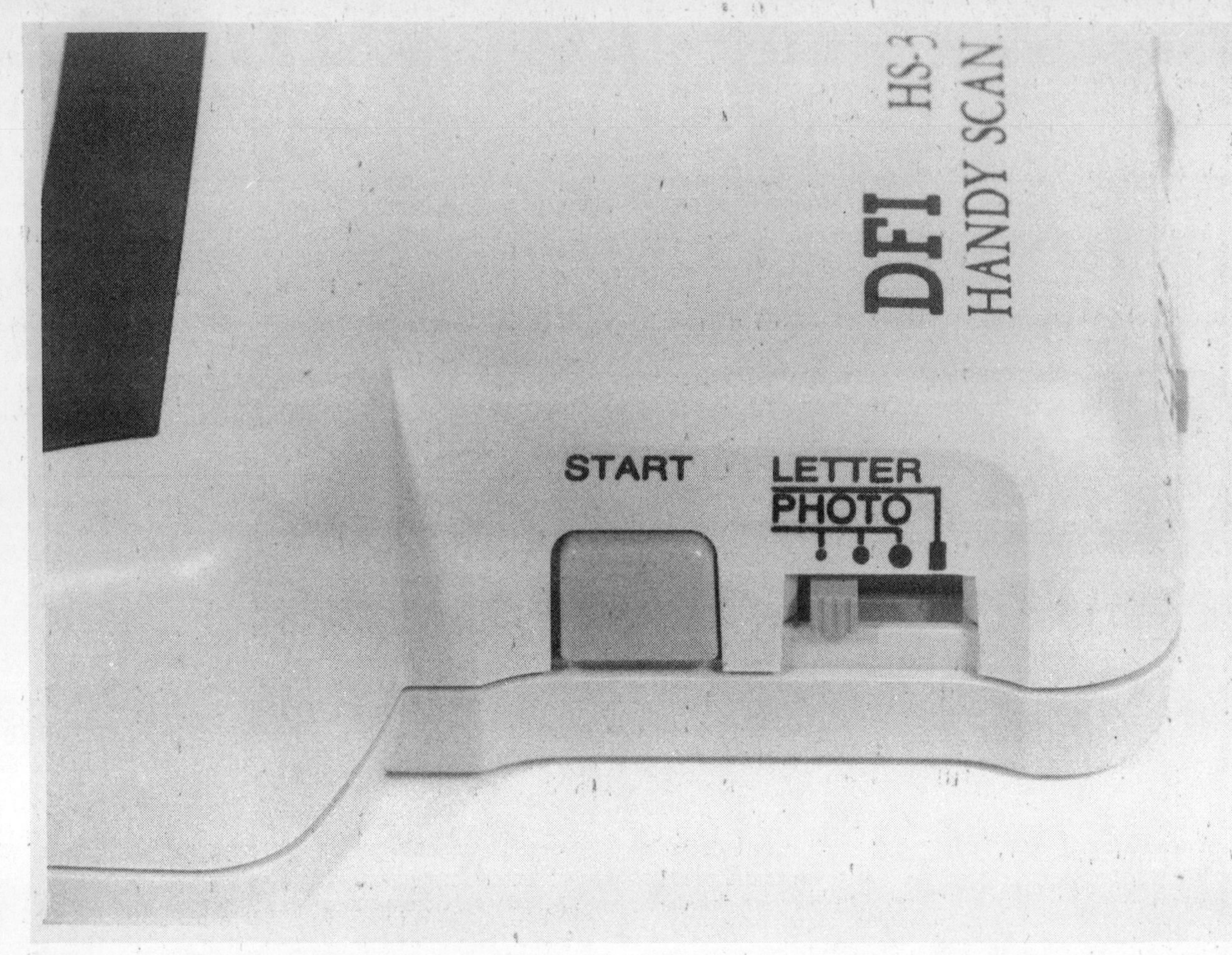

Fig. 5.2 A hand scanner: the start and dither controls

detail the scanner can record.

The majority of scanners allow the user to select from a number of dot-pitches. The highest and lowest pitches the Authors have come across are 75 and 400 d.p.i. It may be thought that the higher the dot-pitch the better, but in fact this is not necessarily so. In practice, the lower pitches can be equally, or even more, useful.

Sheet-fed and flat-bed scanners normally have a basic pitch of 200 d.p.i. This is the standard pitch for use with OCR software. They may in addition offer a lower pitch of 150 or 100 d.p.i., or, rarely, as low as 75 d.p.i. A higher pitch of 300 d.p.i. is also common, to match the resolution of laser printers. There is at least one flat-bed scanner with a resolution of 400 d.p.i., and also at least one model with a resolution of 180 d.p.i., to match 24-pin dot-matrix printers and the Hewlett-Packard PaintJet.

Hand scanners most commonly offer a range of 100, 200 and 300 d.p.i., with the latest types also including 400 d.p.i. There are also some low-price models which offer only 200 d.p.i., and also only a single set of dither patterns. Figure 5.6 shows the pitch setting control on a hand scanner.

Some people have the impression that the scanning pitch must always match the dot-pitch of the printer to be used. This is not correct. Using the dot-pitches allows you some control of the size of the reproduced picture, relative to the size of the original. As each scanned dot will reproduce as one printed dot, if you scan at 300 d.p.i. and use a 300 d.p.i. laser printer, the reproduction will be the same size as the original. If you scan at 150 d.p.i., however, the reproduction will be half the size of the original. On the other hand, if you scan at 300 d.p.i. and use a 180 d.p.i. dot-matrix printer, the reproduction will be *larger* than the original, in the ratio of 5 : 3.

The ability to magnify in this way is useful if you have only a hand scanner and want to produce large-size illustrations. By scanning at 400 d.p.i., if you have a 180 d.p.i. printer you can more than double the size of the original, so that a full A4 page illustration can be produced from an ordinary enprint (4" x 6"). Providing the enprint is reasonably sharp, the quality should be acceptable.

With dithered originals, this is the only method of scaling which should be considered. Most d.t.p. programs do allow scaling of bit-images to fit a frame, but this is done in a relatively crude way. If an image needs to be reduced by 10 per cent in one direction, all that happens is that every tenth row of dots is

Fig. 5.3 A "dithered" scanned photograph

omitted. If an image is to be scaled up by 10 per cent, every tenth row is doubled. It can be seen that this will have a disastrous result on the carefully designed dither patterns, and will result in all-too-obvious lines and patterns on the picture. Figure 5.7 shows a dithered photograph both reproduced dot-for-dot and scaled down. The effect of the crude scaling is obvious. Note that this does not apply to images scanned as line-art. Figure 5.8 shows a photograph scanned in this way. It can be scaled up and down at will. Of course, not all subjects are suitable for this graphic treatment.

Desktop publishing programs differ in the ease with which they allow the size of a scanned image to be maintained. Most will automatically scale an imported image to fit the frame it is assigned to. Timeworks DTP is one of the best in this respect, as it allows whole pixel scaling to be specified for a frame. When this is done, the picture will not be scaled down from its original size. If the picture, as imported, is too big to fit in the frame, you will get a warning that the frame is too small for whole pixel scaling. You can then increase the size of the frame until it will fit.

Where the frame is much larger than the picture, no scaling up will occur until the frame is large enough to allow the picture to be doubled in size, so that every row of dots is printed twice. The next step will be where every pixel can be trebled, and so on. Between these steps, the picture is centred in the frame, with white space left around it. The only problem here is that the two directions are treated separately, so it is possible for the aspect ratio of the picture to be distorted if the frame is large enough, for instance, to allow doubling in one direction but not the other.

With other programs, it may be necessary to calculate how big the reproduced picture should be, and to draw the frame to exactly this size. Obviously, this is not a particularly easy procedure, but it is simplified

Fig. 5.4 As Figure 5.3, but fine dot-screen setting

if you have a printer and a scanner which work at the same pitch. The reproduction will then be the same size as the original.

When viewing scanned images on the screen with a d.t.p. program, remember that these programs always work at printer resolution, and that what you see on the screen is not a pixel-for-dot representation of what will be printed. The screen pixels are much larger than the final printer dots, and this means that the screen quality of dithered images may be quite poor. If you are worried about the final quality, try a test print. Don't judge the quality of an image from what you see on the screen. Figure 5.9 is a screen dump, showing Figure 5.3 being produced.

It should be understood that you cannot produce more detail in the reproduction by scanning at a finer dot-pitch and then scaling the image down in the d.t.p. program. The limit on the detail which can be shown is set by the printer pitch. The best quality will always be obtained by ensuring that one scan point corresponds exactly to one printer dot.

Scanner Software

When you buy a scanner, of any type, it should be supplied with suitable driver software. As well as providing an interface between the scanner and the computer, this software should allow some control of the scan, and some flexibility of output file format.

The most important thing to check is whether the software for the scanner you intend to buy can generate a file format which your d.t.p. package can import. For some computers, there are well-established standards for image files. For others, there are a great many different formats, with each graphics program seemingly having its own file type. The PC world is particularly bad in this respect, though some formats are finding dominance.

Fig. 5.5 As Figure 5.3 but coarse dot-screen setting

For programs running on IBM PCs and compatibles, there are three major file formats used for scanner graphics. In the GEM world, the most important is the .IMG format. This is used by Timeworks DTP (all versions), the GEM Desktop Publisher, Finesse, and Ventura Publisher (all versions). The .IMG format is quite flexible, being suitable for colour or black-and-white images, and offering various degrees of compression. It is also independent of screen format.

The TIFF (Tagged Image File Format) is used by Aldus Pagemaker, amongst others, and is an example of a file format which crosses machine boundaries. It is used on IBM PCs and also on the Apple Macintosh range. TIFF files can contain either bit-image data or true grey-scale information, for those scanners capable of generating it. Ventura Publisher can also read TIFF files, and uses this format for grey-scale files. Timeworks DTP version 1.2 can read in TIFF image files, but of the bit-image type only. It can not handle grey-scale files.

The other major PC format is .PCX, used by PC Paintbrush, and readable by many d.t.p. programs, including Pagemaker, Timeworks DTP, and Ventura Publisher. It is also usable with many paint programs, which can be used to edit scanned images to some extent.

Windows 3 has introduced the .BMP bit-map format. As Windows 3 is likely to become virtually standard in the PC world over the next few years, this format may become widely used. However, Ventura Publisher for Windows does not recognise it.

Many scanner control programs can produce output in all of these formats, so that you may have a choice of file type to transfer images from scanner to d.t.p. program. As far as the quality of the image is concerned, it probably won't make a blind bit of difference which you use, but some programs can use

Fig. 5.6 A hand scanner: the pitch and density controls

one type more efficiently than the others. With programs running under GEM, it is generally best to use the .IMG format where possible. Of course, TIFF must be used for grey-scale images with Ventura. For Pagemaker, the TIFF format is to be preferred for all types of images.

The area which you scan will not always be the exact area you wish to use. You can crop images after they have been imported into some d.t.p. programs, but this can mean you are importing larger files than necessary. Others do not allow this. A good scanner program will allow you to "cut out" the part of the scanned image you wish to use, and save only that part of the image to disk. This is essential if your d.t.p. program does not allow cropping. Figure 5.10 is a screen-dump from a hand-scanner control program.

Orientation is another problem. If you want to scan a full A4 illustration, it can only be placed in the scanner one way round, but you may want it to appear in your document vertically up a page (portrait orientation), or horizontally across a page (landscape orientation). A good scanner program should allow you to rotate the image before saving it to disk. You may be able to rotate the image by 90 degrees in one direction only, so care may be necessary to ensure you place the original in the scanner correctly, otherwise the rotated version could be upside down! Other programs allow rotation to any orientation, in steps of 90 degrees. (It is unusual to be able to rotate an image within a d.t.p. program, in fact the Authors know of none which provide for it.)

The scanner control program may also allow for editing of the scanned image on a pixel-by-pixel basis. This can be useful for correcting small defects, such as dust spots, on the originals, but be warned that it is not at all easy to use for larger corrections or alterations. For a start, scanned images are much larger than the otherwise similar (in structure) images produced by paint programs, which means that you have a much smaller part of the image showing to work on at any one time. This makes it hard to see exactly what you are doing. The second problem concerns the dither patterns. As stated above, these are very carefully designed, and though they may look random, they are not. Any interference to these patterns can stand out like the proverbial sore thumb! Don't plan on using pixel editing for major retouching of scanned images.

Claims for some hand scanners that images wider than the scan width can be scanned in sections and then joined by the scanner program also need to be treated with circumspection. It would need a miracle to do this without the joins showing.

A final point to check is the size of file which the scanner program can generate. With many, it is limited only by the amount of memory available in the computer, which limits the maximum possible scan size (up to the physical limits of the scanner). However, there is at least one scanner control program which can only save files of a maximum size of 64K in some formats, including .IMG, .PCX and TIFF. This is a very small size for a scan file (where sizes of 150 – 250K are common), and frankly is

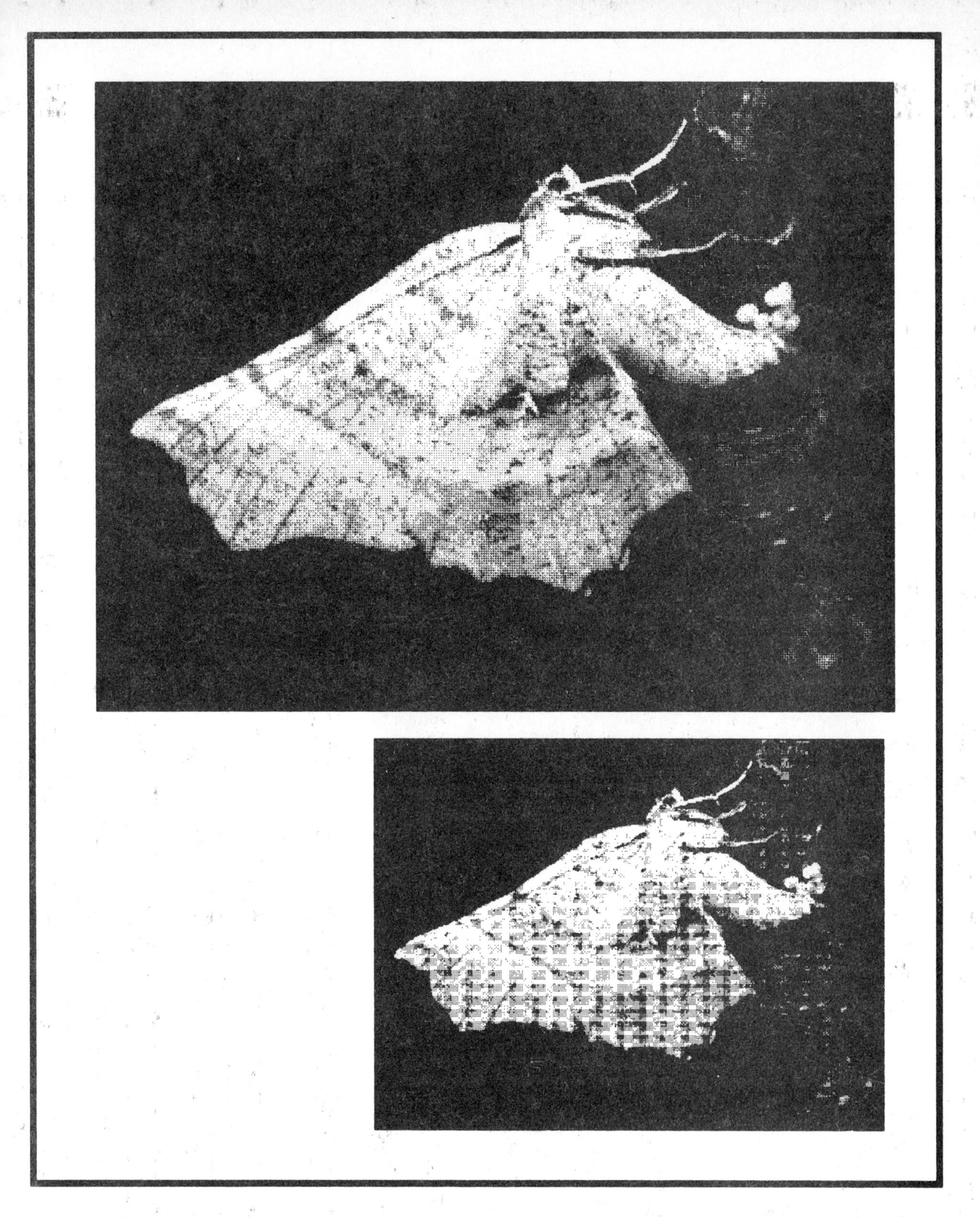

Fig. 5.7 Dithered photograph scaled and unscaled

Fig. 5.8 A photograph scanned on the line setting, scaled and unscaled

Fig. 5.9 Screen dump of a scanned image display

not really usable for serious d.t.p. work.

Which Scanner?

Sheet-feed scanners are primarily designed for use with OCR software for reading in text in printed form. If you intend to do this, then you can also use the scanner for graphics and it would not be worth while considering another type. You would, however, have to put up with the difficulties with scanning some types of artwork.

Flat-bed scanners are undoubtedly the best for scanning all types of graphics. The main problem with them is the expense, and they may be beyond the reach of many. If you need the graphics capability of this type, and also need to scan sheets of text for OCR, it is worth remembering that sheet feeders are available for some flat-bed scanners.

For many people, the inexpensive hand scanners are the only type which can be considered, because of their low price. You should not be misled by this, however. The quality of output they can produce can be excellent, with reasonable operator skill. They can also be used with OCR software. The cost of this software has fallen dramatically in recent times, and some hand scanners are now bundled with a suitable program. This type of scanner is certainly well worth having, and the ability to scan in images from books and other sources physically difficult for other types of scanner, means that it can be worth having one of these even if you have a more expensive type.

When scanning material from books, or other source, you should, of course, remember that it is necessary to obtain permission before reproducing any material which is subject to copyright.

E

Fig. 5.10 A scanner control program

Chapter 6

LAYOUTS AND STYLE SHEETS

In order to place text and graphics on a page, you need some method of specifying where they are to be placed, how many text columns there are to be, and so on. There are two main ways of doing this in d.t.p. Either a system of specifying column dimensions is used, entering the actual sizes usually by some type of fill-in form system, or a system of boxes or "frames" is employed. These are drawn onto the page on the screen, at the size and in the place required.

There are also combinations of these two methods, in various ways. Aldus Pagemaker, for instance, uses column guides for text and a system of frames for graphics. Xerox Ventura Publisher uses frames for graphics, and a system of column guides within the frames for text, with a default frame initially occupying the whole page, and the frame initially containing a single column the full width of the frame. Figure 6.1 is a screen-dump showing the Ventura Margins and Columns dialogue box. Timeworks Desktop Publisher is more consistent in that it uses frames for text and graphics. There are column guides on the Timeworks screen, but these are for guidance in drawing frames only, and you can not place text in them without drawing frames first.

The advantage of the Timeworks method is that it allows you to work entirely visually, placing text and graphics without ever having to deal with actual dimensions. No other d.t.p. program provides quite this degree of freedom. Of course, if you have to work to a predefined layout, where someone has worked out all the column widths, margins, etc., then systems where you type in these dimensions are not at a disadvantage. In fact, it is quite possible to size and place frames in Timeworks by entering actual dimensions (and thereby place frames to an accuracy of 1/100 inch), so in this area this program gives you the best of both worlds.

It is generally up to the operator whether or not the frames and/or column guides are visible on the screen. Programs differ as to whether or not they are displayed by default, but nearly all offer the options of either displaying or hiding them. While actually working on a page, it is normally preferable to have all the frames and guides visible. This helps to prevent overlapping of things which are not intended to overlap, and also gives some idea of the page layout before all the actual items are in place. It is, however, very helpful to be able to preview a page with all the guidelines hidden, to check the layout before printing. Figure 6.2 shows the Ventura screen with the column guides displayed.

There is normally a limit to the number of frames you can have on a page, but it is normally much higher than you would ever want to use, like 100 or so. However, each frame normally takes up some space in memory, and this may set a lower limit. Create too many frames and you may run out of space to do anything with them.

Once the guides and/or frames have been placed, text and graphics can be placed in them. To deal with text first, most d.t.p. programs include basic word processing facilities, so text can be directly entered. However, there may be disadvantages to this with some programs using frames (e.g. Timeworks). When text entered at the keyboard fills a frame, it cannot be made to flow automatically to another (to the next column on the page, for instance). You have to manually move the text cursor to the next frame. Each frame full of text is an entirely separate item to the program, which will not treat them as linked in any way. This makes editing difficult, as if you insert text, any text which overflows from that frame is effectively lost, though, depending on the program, it may reappear if you either enlarge the frame or delete other text from it.

It is normally more convenient to prepare text separately using a word processor program, making sure that the word processor you choose has a file format in common with the d.t.p. program. It is also wise to check how many of the features inserted in the text during word processing are recognised and reserved by the d.t.p. program. These features include such things as emboldening, italicising and underlining. A d.t.p. program may be more compatible with one word processor than with another.

If you have difficulties with compatibility, it is worth remembering that most d.t.p. programs (if not all) can import straight ASCII files, and that most word processors can save files in this format. However, when this is done no features such as underlining can be included in the text.

A text file imported from a word processor can be made to flow from frame to frame, or column to column, in most programs. Subsequent editing is also possible. As you insert text, all the text below it moves down, flowing to the next frame or column where necessary. The only point you have to check is whether any of the text has flowed out of the last frame in the document.

When a text file is imported into Ventura with the default frame active, it is automatically placed on the first free page, filling up the columns in top-to-bottom and left-to-right order, and new pages are added to the document as necessary, without any action being necessary on the user's part. Timeworks, on the other hand, will only place text in the active frame. Otherwise, the text must be placed into frames manually, using the mouse to select the frames. Timeworks will keep the text in order from page to page, but the order of text flow between frames on one page depends on the order in which the frames are selected. This also allows some frames to be left empty, perhaps to be used subsequently for headings or graphics. If text is imported into Ventura without the default frame being active, it behaves substantially the same as Timeworks.

Some column-based programs do allow text flow from column to column and page to page as it is entered from the keyboard. If you intend to enter a lot of text in this way (not recommended), you should obviously choose a program of this sort.

@@

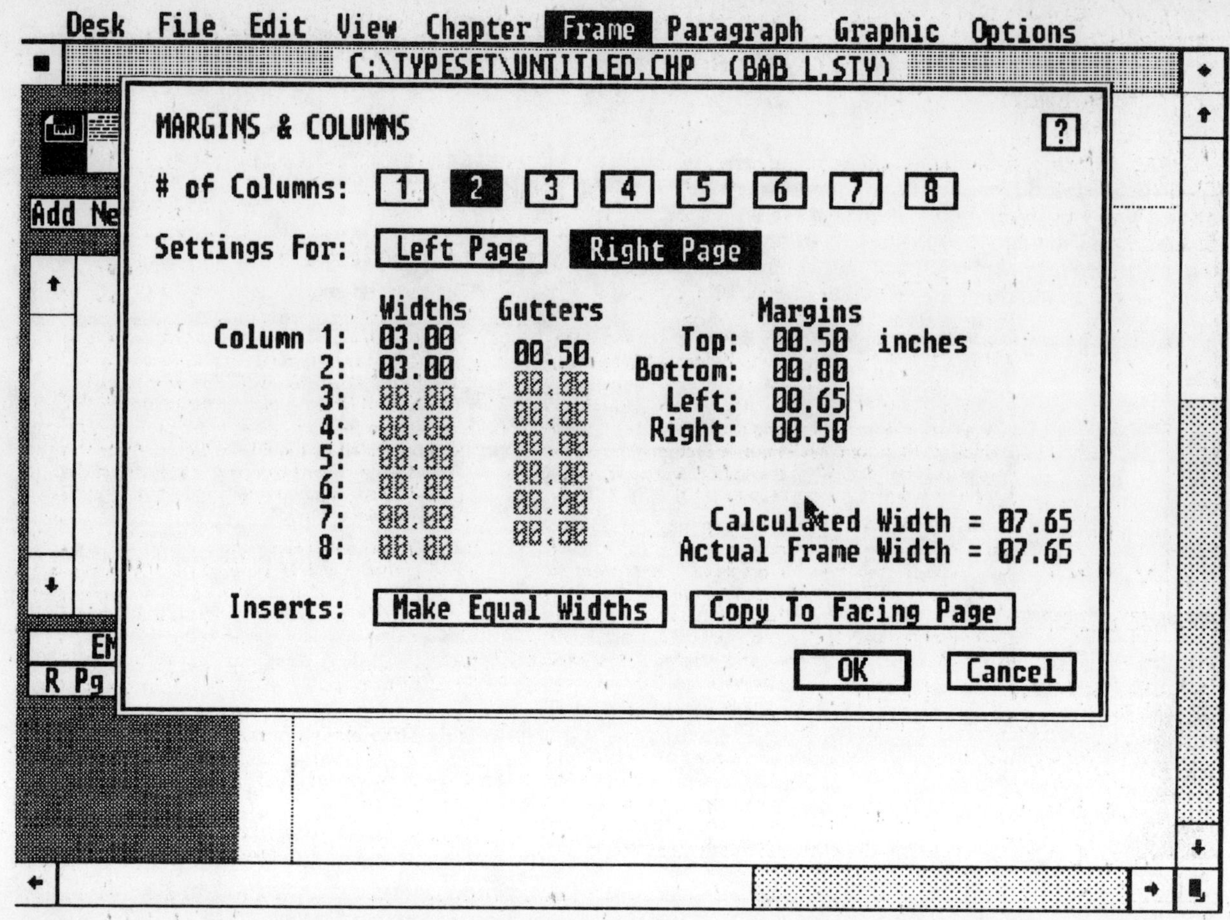

Fig. 6.1 The Ventura Publisher margin and columns dialogue box

When a text file is imported, it may either be copied into the d.t.p. program's document file, or the original text file may be modified and used. Timeworks uses the first system, Ventura the second. The advantage of the Timeworks method is that the original text file is preserved unchanged, but with the disadvantage that the document file can become very large. The Ventura method avoids the generation of very large files, and blocking up disk space with duplicated material, and it also means that the text file can be loaded back into the word processor for further editing (taking care not to corrupt the formatting characters which the d.t.p. program inserts). However, you do have to be careful not to delete the text file while you are still working on the document.

It is sometimes possible to insert the characters used by the d.t.p. program to format the text at the word processing stage. These characters indicate such things as the style to be used for a paragraph. You can, therefore, indicate that a paragraph is to be body text, or a headline, or subheading at the word processing stage, and when the text file is imported into the d.t.p. program, the paragraphs will take these styles automatically. This avoids having to go through the text and change them to appropriate styles one by one. This can be a great time saver, but not all d.t.p. programs have this facility.

Adding Graphics

Like text, graphics can often be drawn within the d.t.p. program, or imported from a paint or draw program which has a file format in common with the d.t.p. program. As with text, the latter course is normally the preferable one.

Desktop publishing programs can often import a wide variety of graphics formats, for both bit-image graphics and vector graphics. The former are normally generated by "paint" programs, and the latter by "draw" or CAD programs. Whenever possible, it is best to use a graphics program which is directly supported by your d.t.p. program. However, there are also a number of conversion programs extant, which will convert from one graphics format to another. These programs can not be said to be trouble free. Some are quite choosy about what they will convert, others may completely fail with some files, but be completely successful with others. With vector graphics especially, some parts of the illustration may not be converted, but simply omitted, so you do need to check after importation to make sure it is all there.

All graphics within d.t.p. programs are generally contained in some kind of frame. It is by means of this frame that graphics can be moved around the screen and (in most programs) scaled and resized. Most d.t.p. programs do allow graphics to be altered

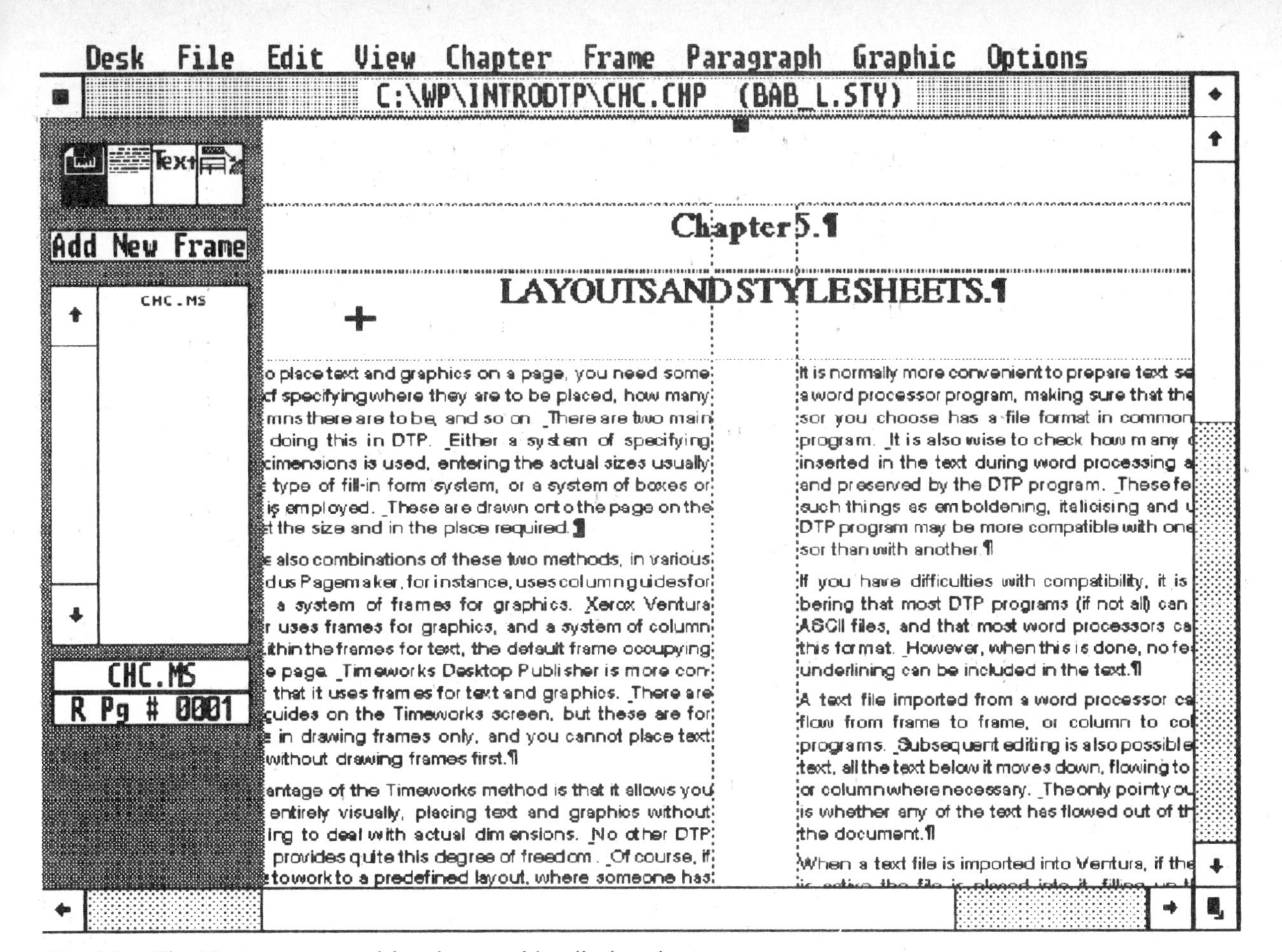

Fig. 6.2 The Ventura screen with column guides displayed

in size, often by simplying resizing the containing frame.

The effectiveness of the scaling depends on the type of the original graphic. In the case of vector graphics, as produced by drawing or CAD type programs, the scaling can be quite sophisticated. However, not all programs have the ability to automatically preserve the aspect ratio of graphics of this type, so care may be necessary to ensure that circles remain truly circular. Other programs will only scale this type of graphic in the correct aspect ratio, so that it will only be possible to completely fill a frame if the frame is drawn the right shape for the illustration.

The main cause of problems with vector graphics is usually any lettering which may be included. In some cases it may be reproduced correctly. In other cases it may appear in quite a different font, or totally the wrong size, or in the wrong place, or both. In general, the best advice is to remove any labels before importing the graphic, and then to relabel it using the d.t.p. program's fonts. This will enable the style of lettering to be consistent with the rest of the document, and will probably also give higher quality, as well as avoiding problems with placement. Depending on the d.t.p. program, you may be able to place text within the graphic's frame, or you may need to use a separate frame for each label.

In the case of bit-image graphics, as produced by drawing type programs, the scaling can only be done in a rather crude way. If a graphic is to be reduced in size by 10 per cent, every tenth row of pixels is simply deleted. An increase in size would be obtained by doubling every tenth row. This can disrupt any fill patterns which have been used, and is also a problem with "dithered" scanner graphics (discussed more fully in Chapter 5). Generally, however, simple line drawings can be scaled without problems.

There should be no problem with lettering in bit-image graphics, except that it is likely to be of very low quality compared to the d.t.p. fonts, and it will also be distorted by scaling. Again, the best answer is to do any labelling with the d.t.p. program after importation, where this is practicable.

Mixing Text and Graphics

Normally, text and graphics will be mixed on the same page, though there may well be pages which are text only, or which have a full-page graphic. The system of frames is used to allow text and graphics to be mixed in an attractive way, but avoiding unintentional overlaps.

The simplest way to mix text and graphics is to draw the frames on the page so that they occupy completely separate areas. However, this may not be possible with those programs which use column guides

(Continued on page 69)

If you have difficulties with compatibility, it is worth remembering that most DTP programs (if not all) can import straight ASCII files, and that most word processors can save files in this format. However, when this is done, no features such as underlining can be included in the text.

A text file imported from a word processor can be made to flow from frame to frame, or column to column, in most programs. Subsequent editing is also possible. As you insert text, all the text below it moves down, flowing to the next frame or column where necessary. The only point you have to check is whether any of the text has flowed out of the last frame in the document.

When a text file is imported into Ventura, if the default frame is active the file is placed into it, filling up the columns in top-to-bottom and left-to-right order, and new pages are added to the document as necessary, without any action being necessary on the user's part. Timeworks, however, will only place text into one frame at a time. It requires that the text is placed in further frames manually, and extra pages must also be added explicitly. Timeworks will keep the text in order from page to page, but the order of text flow between frames on one page depends on the order in which the frames are selected. This also allows some frames to be left empty, perhaps to be used subsequently for headings or graphics. For frames other than the default, Ventura acts substantially the same as Timeworks.

Some column-based programs do allow text flow from column to column and page to page as it is entered from the keyboard. If you intend to enter a lot of text in this way (not recommended), you should obviously choose a program of this sort.

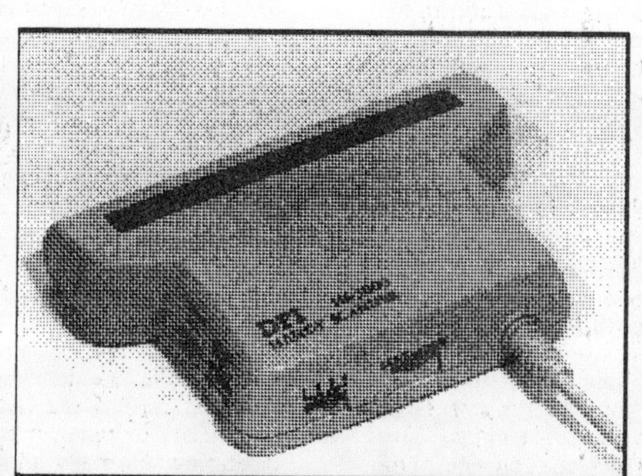

A typical hand scanner.

When a text file is imported, it may either be copied into the DTP program's document file, or the original text file may be modified and used. Timeworks uses the first system, Ventura the second. The advantage of the Timeworks method is that the original text file is preserved unchanged, but with the disadvantage that the document file can disk space with duplicated material, and it also means that the text file can be loaded back into the word processor for further editing (taking care not to corrupt the formatting characters which the DTP program inserts). However, you do have to be careful not to delete the text file while you are still working on the document.

It is sometimes possible to insert the characters used by the DTP program to format the text at the word processing stage. These characters indicate such things as the style to be used for a paragraph. You can, therefore, indicate that a paragraph is to be body text, or a headline, or subheading at the word processing stage, and when the text file is imported into the DTP program, the paragraphs will take these styles automatically. This avoids having to go through the text and change them to appropriate styles one by one. This can be a great time saver, but not all DTP programs have this facility.

Adding Graphics.

Like text, graphics can often either be drawn within the DTP program, or imported from a paint or draw program which has a file format in common with the DTP program. As with text, the latter course is normally the preferable one, as drawing facilities in DTP programs are often primitive and limited.

DTP programs can often import a wide variety of graphics formats, for both bit-image graphics and vector graphics. The former are normally generated by 'paint' programs, and the latter by 'draw' or CAD programs. Whenever possible, it is best to use a graphics program which is directly supported by your DTP program. However, there are also a number of conversion programs extant, which will convert from one graphics format to another. These programs cannot be said to be trouble free. Some are quite choosy about what they will convert, others may complelely fail with some files, but be completely successful with others. With vector graphics especially, some parts of the illustration may not be converted, but simply omitted, so you do need to

Fig. 6.3 A graphic let into a page of text

to place text. There are, however, other methods to ensure that graphics do not obliterate any of the text.

The normal way of preventing text from being hidden is to make the graphics frames "repel" text. In this way, if a graphics frame is placed over text frames or columns, the position of the text will be adjusted so that it "flows" around the frame. Obviously, this will affect the amount of text the column or frame can hold, and so the text below the inserted graphic may have to flow to other frames, and you have to make sure it does not overflow the available space. There can be a particular problem here if the text has been entered from the keyboard in one of those programs which does not allow text of this sort to flow from frame to frame.

The shape of the frame around the graphic is also something which varies from program to program. In some cases the frame can only be rectangular, and text can only be flowed around this rectangular shape. Timeworks is of this type. Other programs, and here Pagemaker is an example, allow the frame to be polygonal, and the text can be flowed around this more complex shape. Whether this is an advantage is a matter of opinion. Where text abuts a sloping edge, and especially where the slope is down from right to left, the text can be difficult to read, and this can become very irritating if overdone. Graphic designers love to do this sort of thing, but its real desirability is debatable.

Figure 6.3 shows a scanned graphic inserted into a page with two columns of text. This example was produced with Ventura, which allows a caption to be attached to the illustration, so that the position of the two can be adjusted together. The amount of "padding", space between the frame and the surrounding text, can also be adjusted.

It is also possible for frames to be set so that they do not repel text. This can be used to allow text and graphics to be deliberately superimposed, but the background "tint" of the frame must also be considered. Most frames will have an opaque background by default. This means that any text passing behind the white areas of the graphic will be hidden. However, if the background can be set to transparent, the text will "show through". There is one point of warning to be given here. Though d.t.p. programs may have these capabilities, not all printers do. The problem is mostly with those which use some form of page compilation or page description language. These may not be able to cope with superimposition, or may place restrictions on it.

On those programs which only allow rectangular frames, it is sometimes possible to flow text around a complex shape by making the main frame containing the graphic non-repelling, and then drawing a series of overlapping, empty, but repelling frames over the graphic to clear the text from behind it. This can, however, be a lot of work, and you need to be sure of the capabilities of your printer here also.

When labelling an illustration after importing it, some programs do allow text to be added to the illustration directly, in its frame. Others will not allow text and graphics to be mixed, or will only allow text to be placed in a frame starting at the top left. In these cases, the labels must each be placed in their own frames, which are drawn overlapping the graphic. These frames must obviously be non-repelling, or the text could not be inserted. They will need to be transparent also, if they pass over any part of the graphic.

Decorative Features

Apart from actual graphics, most d.t.p. programs can produce decorative features on the page. These may include rules, boxes, tints, and possibly others.

Rules are simply straight lines drawn on the page. In d.t.p. they can commonly be drawn vertically or horizontally, but not diagonally. It may, of course, be possible to produce a diagonal rule by drawing it in a frame as a graphic item. Timeworks treats all rules as graphics items in this way. Rules are commonly used to separate text columns, or to separate sections of text. They can also be used to underline headings (though this can appear fussy if overdone), and to separate the top of pages, containing the headings, from the body of the page, containing the text. When this is done, it is often advisable, to maintain balance, to rule off the bottom of the page as well.

Rules can often be drawn in several different widths, from a hairline to decidedly bold, and double or triple rules are also possible. Rules are more commonly used in things like newspapers and journals, where text is fairly densely set than in books, where it is more usual to separate columns by allowing extra space between them.

Boxes are like rules, but run around all four sides of a text item or a graphic. In d.t.p. they often take the form of a border around the containing frame. As with rules, the box line can be of one of several widths, and often single, double, or triple. Since the box will be the size of the frame, it is important to adjust the frame to the size which will give the best appearance on the page, ensuring that there is not too much surplus space in the frame below the text, for example. An exception to this would be if you were boxing all the body text columns in a publication and you wanted the boxes on all the pages to be the same size.

Boxes are most often used to highlight paragraphs of particular importance or interest. They can also be used to enclose headings. A "box out" is a common technique in magazine publishing. Here, a quotation, normally an eye-catching one, taken from the text of the article, is placed in a box and printed in a larger type size than the body text (often in italics). The idea is that the box-out catches the eye of anyone casually flicking through the magazine, and intrigues them sufficiently to cause them to read the full article. It goes without saying that in some publications the box-out quotes are frequently of a provocative or mildly salacious nature!

With graphics frames, and particularly with scanned graphics, it can be a good idea to put a thin line around the frame. This helps to delimit the picture, and to separate it from its surroundings.

Tints are a pattern of fine dots which form a background to (usually) a frame. Like boxing, this makes the frame stand out from the rest of the text, and it can be used for the same purposes as, or in conjunction with, boxing. The tint is normally controllable in stages, expressed in percentages, from

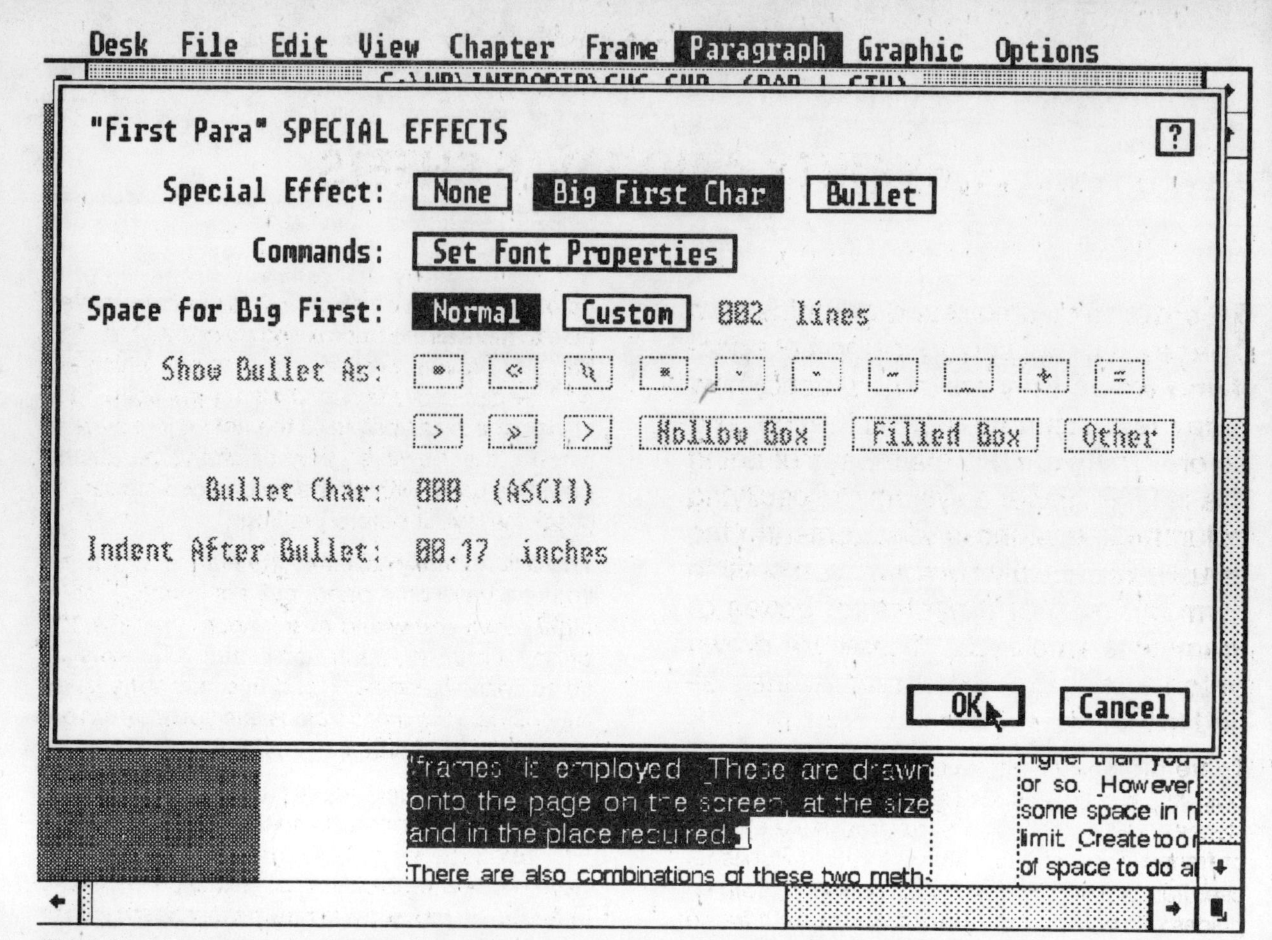

Fig. 6.4 The Ventura special effects dialogue box

very light to black. Care must be used with tints around the middle of the range, as they can make the text difficult to read, unless a large font size is employed. With dark tints, of course, the text will normally be printed in white. Before using white on dark text, you should test your printer's capabilities, as it is not possible to print this on all types. Tint effects may not be very pleasant on low-resolution (dot matrix) printers.

Other decorative features are mostly concerned with text. Some programs can generate outline letter forms from standard fonts, though this is a feature which is frequently only implemented on 68000 based computers like the Macintosh and Atari ST, and not on the less powerful PCs.

It is common practice to in some way enhance the first paragraph of a feature. There are several ways in which this is done. The first word, or line, of the graphic may be printed in a larger and/or emboldened form of the body text font, or the whole paragraph may be printed in a larger size, or with extra leading. Most of these can be done with standard d.t.p. facilities. However, the most popular way is to print the first letter of the paragraph in a very large size, perhaps matching the headline font. Ventura and some other programs have a built-in feature to do this, and the vertical placing of the "big cap" is adjustable. If it is adjusted so that the top is aligned with the tops of the rest of the first line, it is called a "drop cap". This is the most popular style. Figure 6.4 shows the Ventura dialogue box for this feature.

On programs which do not have this facility, it is generally possible to produce a drop cap by putting the first letter in a frame of its own. This frame can then be positioning so that the letter is aligned as required. It will usually be necessary to delete the first letter in the body text to prevent it being printed twice.

Aligning the big cap with the rest of the text may not be that easy. Timeworks, for instance, insists on having quite a bit of extra space around text in a frame. This makes it hard to get the big cap close enough to the text. Firstly, the big cap needs to be given its own paragraph style, with leading and all spaces around the paragraph reduced to the minimum the program will allow. Secondly, justification should be set to range right (i.e. justified right margin, ragged left). The actual frame needs to be made as small as possible, but note that if you make it too small, the letter in it will simply not be printed (or displayed on the screen). The final problem is that what you see on the screen is not necessarily exactly what will be printed on the page. It will be necessary to proof-print the page, possibly several times, in order to align the letter satisfactorily.

More than one of these first-paragraph features

(Continued on Page 72)

Chapter 5.

LAYOUTS AND STYLE SHEETS.

In order to place text and graphics on a page, you need some method of specifying where they are to be placed, how many text columns there are to be, and so on. There are two main ways of doing this in DTP. Either a system of specifying column dimensions is used, entering the actual sizes usually by some type of fill-in form system, or a system of boxes or 'frames' is employed. These are drawn onto the page on the screen, at the size and in the place required.

There are also combinations of these two methods, in various ways. Aldus Pagemaker, for instance, uses column guides for text and a system of frames for graphics. Xerox Ventura Publisher uses frames for graphics, and a system of column guides within the frames for text, the default frame occupying the whole page. Timeworks Desktop Publisher is more consistent in that it uses frames for text and graphics. There are column guides on the Timeworks screen, but these are for guidance in drawing frames only, and you cannot place text in them without drawing frames first.

The advantage of the Timeworks method is that it allows you to work entirely visually, placing text and graphics without ever having to deal with actual dimensions. No other DTP program provides quite this degree of freedom. Of course, if you have to work to a predefined layout, where someone has worked out all the column widths, margins, etc., then systems where you type in these dimensions are not at a disadvantage. In fact, it is quite possible to size and place frames in Timeworks by entering actual dimensions (and thereby place frames to an accuracy of 1/100 inch), so in this area this program gives you the best of both worlds.

It is generally up to the operator whether or not the frames and/or column guides are visible on the screen. Programs differ as to whether or not they are displayed by default, but nearly all offer the actually working on a page, it is normally preferable to have all the frames and guides visible. This helps to prevent overlapping of things which are not intended to overlap, and also gives some idea of the page layout before all the actual items are in place. It is, however, very helpful to be able to preview a page with all the guide lines hidden, to check the layout before printing.

Fig. 6.5 An example page layout

There is normally a limit to the number of frames you can have on a page, but it is normally much higher than you would ever want to use, like 100 or so. However, each frame normally takes up some space in memory, and this may set a lower limit. Create too many frames and you may run out of space to do anything with them.

Once the guides and/or frames have been placed, text and graphics can be placed in them. To deal with text first, most DTP programs include basic word processing facilities, so text can be directly entered. However, there may be disadvantages to this with some programs using frames (e.g. Timeworks). When text entered at the keyboard fills a frame, it cannot be made to flow automatically to another (to the next column on the page, for instance). You have to manually move the text cursor to the next frame. Each frame full of text is an entirely separate item to the program, which will not treat them as lnked in any way. This makes editing difficult, as if you insert text, any text which overflows from that frame is effectively lost, though, depending on the program, it may reappear if you either enlarge the frame or delete other text from it.

It is normally more convenient to prepare text separately using a word processor program, making sure that the word processor you choose has a file format in common with the DTP program. It is also wise to check how many of the features inserted in the text during word processing are recognised and preserved by the DTP program. These features include such things as emboldening, italicising and underlining. A DTP program may be more compatible with one word processor than with another.

Chapter 5.

Layouts and Style Sheets.

In order to place text and graphics on a page, you need some method of specifying where they are to be placed, how many text columns there are to be, and so on. There are two main ways of doing this in DTP. Either a system of specifying column dimensions is used, entering the actual sizes usually by some type of fill-in form system, or a system of boxes or 'frames' is employed. These are drawn onto the page on the screen, at the size and in the place required.

There are also combinations of these two methods, in various ways. Aldus Pagemaker, for instance, uses column guides for text and a system of frames for graphics. Xerox Ventura Publisher uses frames for graphics, and a system of column guides within the frames for text, the default frame occupying the whole page. Timeworks Desktop Publisher is more consistent in that it uses frames for text and graphics. There are column guides on the Timeworks screen, but these are for guidance in drawing frames only, and you cannot place text in them without drawing frames first.

The advantage of the Timeworks method is that it allows you to work entirely visually, placing text and graphics without ever having to deal with actual dimensions. No other DTP program provides quite this degree of freedom. Of course, if you have to work to a predefined layout, where someone has worked out all the column widths, margins, etc., then systems where you type in these dimensions are not at a disadvantage. In fact, it is quite possible to size and place frames in Timeworks by entering actual dimensions (and thereby place frames to an accuracy of 1/100 inch), so in this area this program gives you the best of both worlds.

It is generally up to the operator whether or not the frames and/or column guides are visible on the screen. Programs differ as to whether or not they are displayed by default, but nearly all offer the options of either displaying or hiding them. While actually working on a page, it is normally preferable to have all the frames and guides visible. This helps to prevent overlapping of things which are not intended to overlap, and also gives some idea of the page layout before all the actual items are in place. It is, however, very helpful to be able to preview a page with

Fig. 6.6 An example page layout

may be combined. For instance, you might combine a drop cap with printing the whole paragraph in a larger size than the body text. As with so many other aspects of design, one must be careful not to overdo it, however. Figure 6.5 shows a drop cap combined with a large font size for the first paragraph, and Figure 6.6 combines a big cap combined with a larger font size for the first line, on the same baseline.

The Creative Side
Of course, the placing of text and graphics is more than just getting all the material into the document. The way in which a document is laid out can greatly contribute to, or detract from, the effectiveness of the document.

One of the most important things is to be consistent throughout the document. This means using the same basic page layout throughout the document, using the same typefaces and sizes throughout for the same purposes (body text, subheadings, headings, captions), and also using the same approach for inserting illustrations, either aligning them with the

(Continued on Page 74)

Chapter 5.

LAYOUTS AND STYLE SHEETS.

In order to place text and graphics on a page, you need some method of specifying where they are to be placed, how many text columns there are to be, and so on. There are two main ways of doing this in DTP. Either a system of specifying column dimensions is used, entering the actual sizes usually by some type of fill-in form system, or a system of boxes or 'frames' is employed. These are drawn onto the page on the screen, at the size and in the place required.

There are also combinations of these two methods, in various ways. Aldus Pagemaker, for instance, uses column guides for text and a system of frames for graphics. Xerox Ventura Publisher uses frames for graphics, and a system of column guides within the frames for text, the default frame occupying the whole page. Timeworks Desktop Publisher is more consistent in that it uses frames for text and graphics. There are column guides on the Timeworks screen, but these are for guidance in drawing frames only, and you cannot place text in them without drawing frames first.

The advantage of the Timeworks method is that it allows you to work entirely visually, placing text and graphics without ever having to deal with actual dimensions. No other DTP program provides quite this degree of freedom. Of course, if you have to work to a predefined layout, where someone has worked out all the column widths, margins, etc., then systems where you type in these dimensions are not at a disadvantage. In fact, it is quite possible to size and place frames in Timeworks by entering actual dimensions (and thereby place frames to an accuracy of 1/100 inch), so in this area this program gives you the best of both worlds.

It is generally up to the operator whether or not the frames and/or column guides are visible on the screen. Programs differ as to whether or not they are displayed by default, but nearly all offer the options of either displaying or hiding them. While actually working on a page, it is normally preferable to have all the frames and guides visible. This helps to prevent overlapping of things which are not intended to overlap, and also gives some idea of the page layout before all the actual items are in place. It is, however, very helpful to be able to preview a page with all the guide lines hidden, to check the layout before printing.

There is normally a limit to the number of frames you can have on a page, but it is normally much higher than you would ever want to use, like 100 or so. However, each frame normally takes up some space in memory, and this may set a lower limit. Create too many frames and you may run out of space to do anything with them.

Once the guides and/or frames have been placed, text and graphics can be placed in them. To deal with text first, most DTP programs include basic word processing facilities, so text can be directly entered. However, there may be disadvantages to this with some programs using frames (e.g. Timeworks). When text entered at the keyboard fills a frame, it cannot be made to flow automatically to another (to the next column on the page, for instance). You have to manually move the text cursor to the next frame. Each frame full of text is an entirely separate item to the program, which will not treat them as lnked in any way. This makes editing difficult, as if you insert text, any text which overflows from that frame is

Fig. 6.7 An example page layout

It is normally more convenient to prepare text separately using a word processor program, making sure that the word processor you choose has a file format in common with the DTP program. It is also wise to check how many of the features inserted in the text during word processing are recognised and preserved by the DTP program. These features include such things as emboldening, italicising and underlining. A DTP program may be more compatible with one word processor than with another.

If you have difficulties with compatibility, it is worth remembering that most DTP programs (if not all) can import straight ASCII files, and that most word processors can save files in this format. However, when this is done, no features such as underlining can be included in the text.

A text file imported from a word processor can be made to flow from frame to frame, or column to column, in most programs. Subsequent editing is also possible. As you insert text, all the text below it moves down, flowing to the next frame or column where necessary. The only point you have to check is whether any of the text has flowed out of the last frame in the document.

When a text file is imported into Ventura, if the default frame is active the file is placed into it, filling up the columns in top-to-bottom and left-to-right order, and new pages are added to the document as necessary, without any action being necessary on the user's part. Timeworks, however, will only place text into one frame at a time. It requires that the text is placed in further frames manually, and extra pages must also be added explicitly. Timeworks will keep the text in order from page to page, but the order of text flow between frames on one page depends on the order in which the frames are selected. This also allows some frames to be left empty, perhaps to be used subsequently for headings or graphics. For frames other than the default, Ventura acts substantially the same as Timeworks.

Some column-based programs do allow text flow from column to column and page to page as it is entered from the keyboard. If you intend to enter a lot of text in this way (not recommended), you should obviously choose a program of this sort.

When a text file is imported, it may either be copied into the DTP program's document file, or the original text file may be modified and used. Timeworks uses the first system, Ventura the second. The advantage of the Timeworks method is that the original text file is preserved unchanged, but with the disadvantage that the document file can become very large. The Ventura method avoids the generation of very large files, and blocking up disk space with duplicated material, and it also means that the text file can be loaded back into the word processor for further editing (taking care not to corrupt the formatting characters which the DTP program inserts). However, you do have to be careful not to delete the text file while you are still working on the document.

It is sometimes possible to insert the characters used by the DTP program to format the text at the word processing stage. These characters indicate such things as the style to be used for a paragraph. You can, therefore, indicate that a paragraph is to be body text, or a headline, or subheading at the word text columns, or placing them across columns and flowing the text around them, or keeping text and illustrations in separate areas.

One of the first things to be considered is whether the paper will be printed on both sides, or on one side only. In one-sided printing, the blank pages opposite can be ignored, but in two-sided printing, the two facing pages must be considered as a single entity for design purposes. They need to be designed either to provide a symmetrical layout around the central gutter, or to have a harmonious asymmetrical design. The second option is generally the harder to pull off successfully.

Whether single or double sided, you also need to consider the type of binding to be used for the final document. If ring-binding is to be used, sufficient space must be allowed for the punch holes. With plastic channel binders you also need to allow extra space on the inner edges. If a document is to be printed and bound professionally, you should seek the printer's advice on how much binding width to allow.

Readability

One of the most important considerations in any document is readability, and perhaps the most important factor here is the width of the text columns. How wide should a column be? The answer is 65 characters. It may be surprising that such a precise answer can be given, but it is a fact that this does seem to be the optimum for most type sizes, in English at least. If you make columns narrower than this, the text will read jerkily, and there will also be an excessive amount of hyphenation. If wider, readers will tend to "lose their place" as they go from the end of one line to the beginning of the next. If it is essential to use a column width greater than 65 characters, this problem can usually be reduced by increasing the leading, or space between lines, but of course this reduces the amount of text which can be placed on a page. Figure 6.6 is an example of this.

The choice of typeface is also an important factor in readability. Choice of typeface, and also useful combinations of typeface, are fully discussed in Chapter 3.

It is also important to remember that if you insert too many illustrations with text flowed around them, you are in effect narrowing the column width over a major part of the document. If a document contains a lot of illustrations, it is usually preferable to avoid this type of layout. The width of illustrations should be adjusted to the width of a column, or multiple columns, or text and illustrations should be separate vertically (e.g. text at the top of a page, illustration below). Alternatively, text and illustrations can be placed on separate pages.

The spacing between text columns, known as the "gutters", is also important. If too narrow, the eye may tend to try to cross to the next column instead of moving down and across to the start of the next line. Normally, narrower gutters can be used if the text columns are justified on both margins rather than if the right margin is left ragged. Wide gutters can give an attractive, clean-looking page layout, but do, of course, reduce the amount of text to a page.

White Space

The gutters are a part of what is called the "white space" on a page. This is simply blank areas between the text and graphics items. The use of white space plays a major part in the overall appearance of a document.

If very little white space is left, the document will appear crowded, fussy, and difficult to read. We expect you have all seen club newsletters, on cheap duplicating paper, with the typewriter margins set right out to the sides of the paper and the line spacing set to minimum. This is the ideal way to get the maximum number of words on a page and also to ensure that the minimum of them are read. Figure 6.7 shows a layout which is just about acceptable for something like a technical book. The text is closely set in a small point size, and minimal space is allowed for the headings.

If it really is necessary to cram text onto the page, with narrow line spacing, readability can be maintained by keeping the columns and gutters narrow, and making extensive use of fine vertical and horizontal rules to separate them. This is the typical style of newspapers.

Magazines normally use more white space, and generally the more up-market the magazine, the more white space. One should beware of going too far, however. If there is more space than text, the effect is to imply that the text is not very important, and any illustrations become paramount. In fashion magazines this may be quite deliberate, of course.

When setting the dimensions for gutters, etc., you need to be consistent in the vertical and horizontal directions to maintain a balanced appearance. If you increase the space between columns, you also need to increase the vertical space between paragraphs, and perhaps the leading too. You also need to allow more space around any illustrations let into the text.

Paragraph Styles

The ability to predefine paragraph styles is an important tool in maintaining a consistent style throughout a document. "Paragraph" in this context includes such things as headings and subheadings, and captions to illustrations.

Normally, when defining a paragraph, you can set the font (style and size) to be used for that paragraph, together with the leading, and also such things as the left and right margins (the space between the first and last letters on a line and the frame or column guide limits). The spacing between paragraphs can be defined in one of two ways, depending on the program. Either the paragraph always starts at the very top of the available space, and spacing is set by leaving space below the paragraph, or it is done the other way around. You specify the space to be left above the paragraph for each style, and the text will go to the very bottom of the available space.

For headings it is normally possible to have them justified left or right, or centred in the available space (which normally means the frame). Major headings are normally best centred, though there will always be exceptions. The style used for subheadings needs to be considered in conjunction with the body text style. If the body text paragraphs have flush first lines, with only extra space to separate them, we

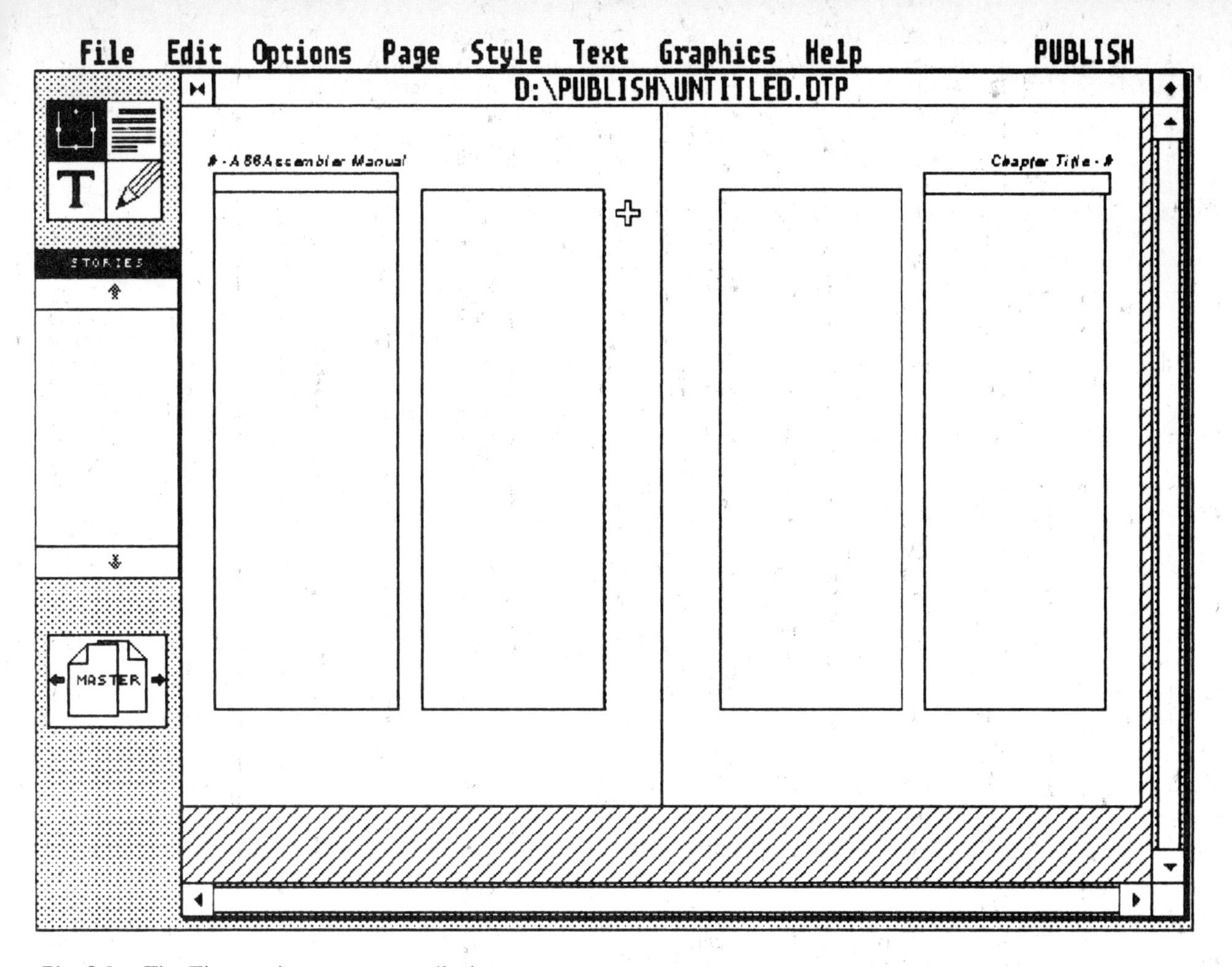

Fig. 6.8 The Timeworks master page display

think the subheadings look best centred within the columns.

Though we talk of headings and subheadings, in many cases it is necessary to have three or more levels of heading, and it is necessary to maintain a hierarchy among them, in order to make their relative importance clear. The easiest way of doing this is by type size. For instance, main headings could be in a large type size, minor subheadings in body text size but emboldened, and major subheadings in an intermediate size.

If this would result in having too many font sizes in the document, the same size can be used for all subheadings, but the major ones can be all in capitals and the minor ones in upper and lower case, or the major subheadings can be underlined.

Main headings can be made to stand out very effectively by making them white against a black background. Most d.t.p. programs have this facility, but some printers may not be able to print it. It is not a good idea to do this for subheadings, however, as it usually breaks the page design up too much, especially if there are several subheadings on a page.

As well as normal indents, most d.t.p. programs can produce hanging indents or "outdents", where the first line begins to the left of the following lines in the paragraph. This can be very effective when used in conjunction with "bullets".

Bullets are round dots, stars, hands or other symbols used as decorative features. They are most commonly used when giving a list of features, for instance in advertising.

With paragraph styles, as with fonts, it is generally a mistake to use too many different ones within one document. The result of doing so is to produce a document which is either messy, or which gives a rather lightweight, sensationalistic impression. You may need up to three or four heading styles, a body text style, and probably two caption styles (for single-line and multi-line captions) if your document is illustrated. You may also need a special style for quotations, usually like body text but more indented, and perhaps a special style for introductory paragraphs, or a bullet style as described above. Think very carefully about using more than this.

Saving Styles

Having developed a style for a document, you may well want to use that style for other, related, documents. It would be a nuisance if you had to do all the work of designing page layouts and specifying paragraph styles again, so most d.t.p. programs have

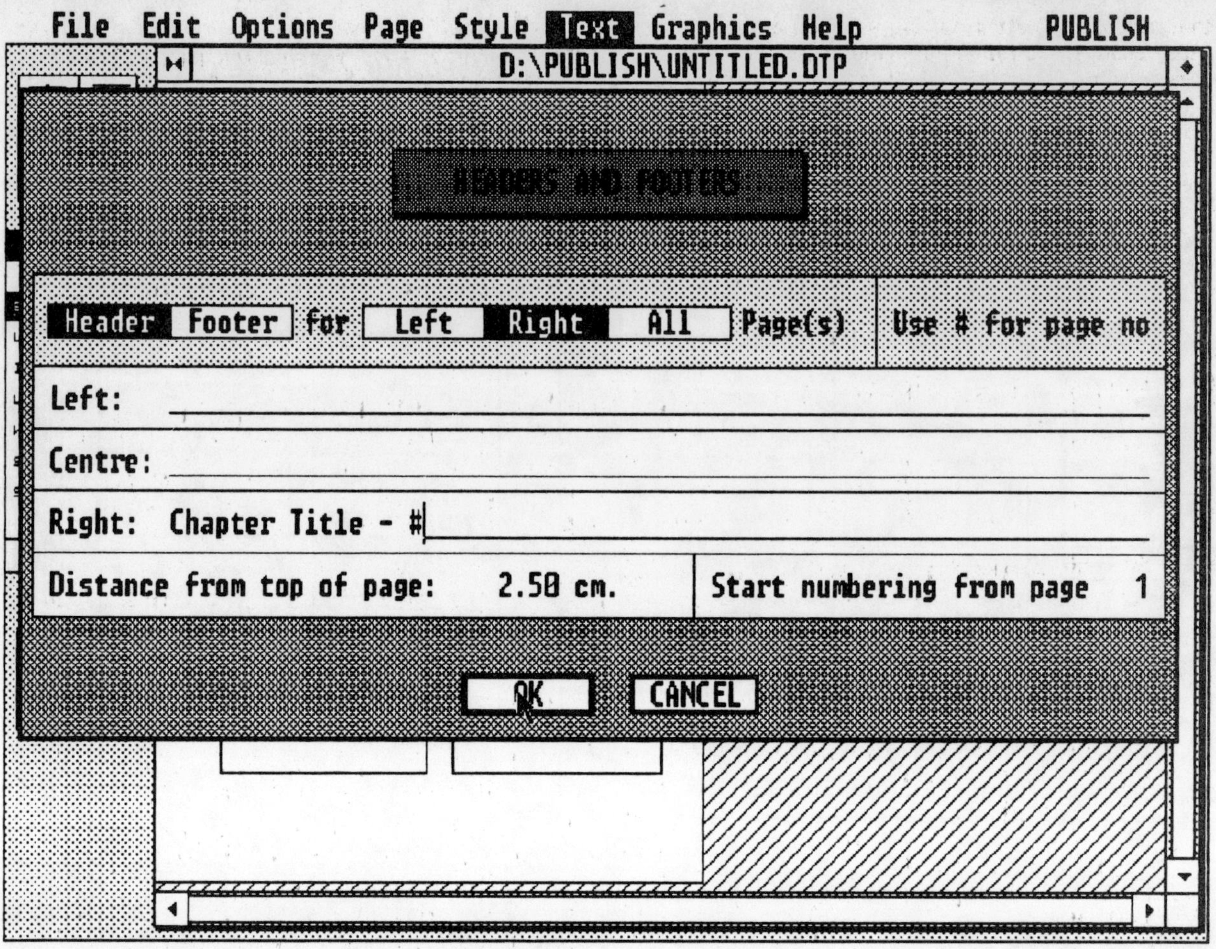

Fig. 6.9 The Timeworks headers and footers dialogue box

some means of allowing the overall design, without text or illustrations, to be saved, as a *style sheet*. Exactly what can be saved does vary slightly from program to program, as does the way in which the saved styles are actually saved or loaded for re-use. A few very simple, beginner's, d.t.p. programs do not have a style sheet facility (for example, Timeworks DTP Lite). Though other programs can and do differ in detail and substance from this, it will give you a good idea of what style sheets are for, and how to use them.

In Timeworks, a system of master pages are used to design the basic page layouts. You can have either a single master page, for documents which will be printed on one side only, or where you want identical layouts on left and right pages, or you can have left and right master pages with differing layouts. You can not have separate master pages for the first page (title page) of a document. This would have to be designed separately for each document using the style. Figure 6.8 shows the Timeworks screen with the master pages for a two-page layout displayed. There are two text columns on each page, together with running headers.

On the master page you can put virtually anything which can be included in a document. This can include the frames which hold text and graphics, rules and boxes, and running headers and footers. In fact, headers and footers can only be specified by using the master pages. All these can be different for the left and right hand pages, so, for instance, you could have the book title as the header on one side and the chapter name and number as the header on the other. Automatic page numbering can be included in the header or footer (or both, should you so desire). Figure 6.9 shows the Timeworks dialogue box for setting a running header.

It is possible to include substantial text or graphics in the master pages, but as this would appear identically on all pages in the document, it is something that would not be done very often. The ability to include a small symbol, device or logo could be useful, however, as could the ability to include running text longer than the single line allowed in a header or footer.

When working on a document, each time you add a page to it, the new page initially takes on the form of the master page, with the frames there ready to take text or illustrations. It is, however, possible to alter or remove any of the master page features from individual pages, so the use of master pages does not involve any loss of flexibility. One point you need to check is whether, if you make an alteration to the master pages after starting work on a document, those changes are reflected in the pages already produced. In Timeworks they are not. You will probably need to find out by experiment, as instructions rarely mention this point.

As well as the master page features, other things are included in the style sheet. These include all the defined paragraph styles, which are the other main ingredient in the look of a document. The style sheet is saved as a disk file, by selecting the Save Style option from the File menu. Generally, the style sheet will be given the same name as the document you are working on, but with a special extension, such as .STY. You can specify a different name if you wish, but the extension is normally mandatory or the program will not recognise the file.

When you create a new document you are given the option of loading a style sheet. When you do so the master page design is loaded, and the pages of your new document will take that style and all the paragraph styles will also appear ready for use.

Glossary

ACCESS TIME. The time taken to get data from store into the computer ready for use. Access time is less from a RAM disk than from a hard disk, and less from a hard disk than from floppy disks.

ALPHANUMERIC. Data containing a mixture of alphabetical characters and numbers. Most text is alphanumeric to some extent. It is also used to describe keyboards which have both letter and number characters, as distinct from numeric keypads.

AMPERSAND. This is the symbol "&", normally used in printing as an abbreviation for "and".

ANTIQUE PAPER. An uncoated paper, usually fairly heavy, with a rough, textured surface. It is also frequently off-white or pale tinted.

ARABIC NUMERALS. The standard form of numerals, i.e. 1, 2, 3, 4, 5, 6, 7, 8 and 9, as distinct from Roman numerals, made up from the letters I, V, X, M, C and others.

ART PAPER. A high quality fairly heavy paper designed to take half-tone letterpress reproductions. It is a coated paper with a glossy or very glossy surface.

ARTWORK. Graphics material in colour or black-and-white intended for reproduction, but not including photographs. The term *mechanicals* is used in the USA.

ASCENDER. The part of a lower-case letter which extends above the body of the letter, up to the height of a capital letter. The letters b, d, h (among others) have ascenders while a, e and x do not.

ASCII. American Standard Code for Information Interchange. Pronounced "askey". This is the standard code for representing alphanumeric characters by numeric values within computers, and for sending text information between them. As well as representations of the alphanumeric characters, it also includes "control codes" for line feed, carriage return, etc.

ASTERISK. The star symbol "*". This is normally used as a reference to a footnote. Note that in printing the asterisk is normally placed high on the line, going wholly or partially above the top line of the lettering. Computer printers normally place the asterisk at mid-height on the line.

BACKING UP. This means printing the second side of a sheet. Whenever possible this is done so that the line positions on the two sides match. This gives a cleaner result, with less text showing through from the other side.

BACKS. The page margin nearest to the fold.

BANNER. In a newspaper this means a main headline running across the top of a page. Nowadays (especially in the tabloid press) it also implies the use of an extra-large font size. In magazines, it is sometimes used to mean the title of the magazine on the front cover.

BASELINE. The line on which both capital letters and lower case letters stand. Any part of a character extending below the baseline is a descender (q.v.).

BEZIER CURVE. A form of curve used in some drawing programs which is said to be excellent for drawing "real world" objects. The characteristics of the curve are controlled by the lengths and directions of two lines.

BINDING. The cover of a book, excluding any dust jacket.

BIT IMAGE. An illustration in the form of a regular matrix of dots, each of which may be printed or not printed. Each dot corresponds to one binary digit (bit) in the digital electronic form of the illustration.

BIT MAP. A form of storing fonts in digital form, where each character is made up of a pattern of dots, stored as bit images (q.v.).

BLACK. A heavy version of a typeface, heavier than bold.

BLEED. The practice of extending illustrations, solids, rules and tones beyond the final dimensions of the printed page to make trimming easier. It also means any extra area included in illustrations or photographs for this purpose.

BLOBS. Solid black disks, normally used as bullets (q.v.).

BODY. The space, measured from top to bottom, on which a letter is set.

BODY TEXT. The main text of a story, as distinct from headings and captions. In d.t.p., Body Text is normally the default paragraph style.

BOLD. A heavy version of a typeface.

BOLTS. The edges of folded paper before trimming.

BOOK. The medium weight of a typeface, intended for body text. This term is mostly used in the USA.

BOWL. The rounded part of letters such as P, B, d and b.

BOX. A continuous rule around all four sides of a block of text (*boxed text*).

BRACES. The "curly brackets" { }.

BRACKETS. The "square brackets" [ ] .

BROADSHEET. A large-size newspaper (as distinct

from a *tabloid*), or documents this size. Pedantically, it refers to anything printed on a full-size sheet of paper.

BRUSH. A paint program term, which refers to the notional implement with which the paintings are produced. This can be anything from a small round area of a single colour, to a large irregular shape in multiple colours which gives special effects.

BUFFER. A temporary storage area, either a block of memory in the computer or memory in a device such as a printer, which is used to compensate for differences in speed between devices. Data is sent to the buffer, where it waits until the receiving device can use it.

BULK. The thickness of the sheets of paper making up a document.

CAD/CAM. Computer Aided Design or Drawing / Computer Aided Manufacture. Drawings produced using CAD programs can generally be imported into d.t.p. programs and used for illustrative purposes, provided the two programs have a mutual file format.

CALLIGRAPHIC. Describes a typeface design based on classical handwritten letter forms, e.g. Zapf Chancery.

CANNON BALLS. Solid disks, the same as blobs.

CAP HEIGHT. The height of capital letters in a font, normally expressed in points.

CAPTION. Text describing, or giving the context of, an illustration.

CENTREFOLD. A picture (especially a photograph) taken across most of the width of a centre spread. Especially used to refer to photographs of scantily-clad women.

CENTRE-SPREAD. The centre pages in a folded publication, or in a folded section, where the paper presents a continuous surface equal to two pages.

CHARACTER. An individual letter, figure or symbol in a type font.

COATED PAPER. A paper with one or both surfaces finished with a layer of China Clay or Baryta. This gives a smooth-surface paper, particularly suited to half-tone or colour reproduction.

COLLATING. The gathering and arranging of the sheets or sections of a publication in the correct order for binding.

COLOPHON. The production details of a document.

COLUMN RULE. A fine vertical rule used to separate columns of text.

CONTINUOUS TONE. Reproduction of illustrations including shades as well as black and white. Continuous tone or contone is normally used to describe a photographic print which, when screened, becomes a half-tone.

COPY. The original form of text, manuscript or typescript, from which text is to be typeset. In d.t.p. it can also mean making a duplicate of a disk file. In computing, **Hard Copy** means anything printed out on paper, as distinct from on disk or in memory.

CORRECTION MARKS. A set of standard symbols used by printers, proof readers, designers and authors to indicate changes to be made in a document in proof form.

COVER. The outside pages of a document. The binding of a book. The dust-jacket of a book.

CROPPING. Cutting an illustration to fit the area available, or to remove extraneous material.

CROSS REFERENCE. A reference to text within the same document with relevance to the current text.

CROSSHEAD. A centred subheading.

CURRENT DIRECTORY. Most disk filing systems use a hierarchical file structure, with directories and subdirectories to divide files into groups. The current directory is the directory within this structure that the program will use by default, that is, unless it is instructed to use a different directory.

CUT OUT. A photograph from which the background has been painted out, leaving the subject in isolation.

DECKLE. The uneven, uncut edge of a mould-made or hand-made paper. It is also sometimes used to refer to a torn edge.

DELETE. To erase or remove.

DESCENDER. The part of lower-case letters such as q, g and y, which extends below the baseline. The only upper-case letter with a descender is Q (though the G may also have one in some calligraphic italic forms).

DIGITISING. Converting text or illustrations into a digital, machine-readable form. Digitised text may be included in a document by use of Optical Character Recognition software (OCR). Digitised illustrations may be included directly as bit-images (q.v.).

DINGBAT. A decorative symbol, similar to a bullet but normally larger and more complex. The best known are the Zapf Dingbats, which are available in electronic form for many d.t.p. programs. Dingbats is a registered trade mark of the International Typeface Corporation.

DIRECTORY. In a disk filing system, files are divided up into directories and subdirectories. A directory is therefore a part of a disk which contains files, and possibly further subdirectories. (Note however that a directory is not necessarily a contiguous physical area on the disk.)

DISPLAY. In d.t.p. this means the computer VDU screen. In text, it means large or ornate fonts not normally used for body text. In layout, it refers to the use of such fonts, together with rules, boxing and other visual devices.

DITHERING. The simulation of half-tones in a bit-image (q.v.), by varying the number of dots printed in different areas of the image.

DONGLE. A hardware device which usually plugs into one of the computer's ports, and which is necessary in order to use a program with which it is supplied. It is a security device, intended to prevent illicit copying and use of the program. Few dongled programs have reached a high level of commercial success!

DROP. The vertical distance from the chapter title to the first line of body text.

DROP CAP. A large capital letter at the start of a paragraph, with its top edge aligned with the top edge of the first line of text in the paragraph. Commonly used as a decorative feature at the beginning of a story.

DROP SHADOW. A tint below and to one side of an illustration or piece of text to give a shadow effect.

DRY TRANSFER. Rub-down lettering or symbols, etc., used in the preparation of artwork.

DUST JACKET. A paper cover around the binding of a book, mostly protective, but often carrying an illustration, and also the publisher's "blurb" and biographical details of the author.

EM. The square of the body of a type. An "em space" is a space equal in width to a lower-case "m". Letter spacing, word spacing and kerning are often expressed in em units.

EMS. A form of expanded memory on IBM and compatible computers. See Expanded Memory.

EN. Half the square of the body of a type. An "en space" is a space equal to the width of a lower-case "n".

END PAPER. The leaves that join the binding (cover) of a book to the text, often of a coloured or decorative paper.

EXPANDED. A wider version of a typeface.

EXPANDED MEMORY. Extra memory fitted into a computer, usually on plug-in cards, which enables more data to be held in memory at one time. This can be of great advantage in d.t.p. *provided the program is able to utilise it.* Note that in IBM PC and compatible computers, expanded memory and extended memory refer to two entirely separate things. Some programs can use one but not the other.

EXTENDED MEMORY. In an IBM PC or compatible computer, this is extra memory above the normal 640K DOS limit. It is not the same as expanded memory. See Expanded Memory above.

FAMILY. A set of typefaces with similar design characteristics in different weights. A set of closely-related typefaces. A set of differing typefaces derived from a common ancestor.

FOLIO. A page. A page number.

FOOT. The bottom margin on a page.

FOOTER. A running heading printed in or immediately above the foot of every page in a document (e.g. carrying the page number).

FOREDGE. The outer vertical edge of a page.

FORMAT. The size of a document (page size). The orientation of pages (i.e. vertical format, horizontal format). The arrangement of text and headings on a page.

FONT. The complete character set of a particular typeface in a particular size and style. In d.t.p., the target device (i.e. screen, printer) may also be included in the specification. Sometimes incorrectly used as a synonym for typeface. This should be avoided as "font" as a term distinct from "typeface" is indispensible. Pedantry here is fully justified!

FOUNT. The same as "font". Still used in the UK, but obsolescent.

FULL OUT LEFT. Text which is set out to the full left margin of a column, without indentation. Left-justified text.

FULL POINT. A full stop (.) .

GALLEY PROOFS. Text proofs in the form of a continuous single column, not paginated.

GATE FOLD. A single sheet of paper with two vertical folds, making six pages.

GATHER. To assemble the pages of a document in order. The same as "collate".

GRAIN. The direction in which machine-made paper is made, and along which it will fold and tear most readily. Hand-made and mould-made papers may have no discernible grain.

GRAPHICS. Display material made up of lines and (or) dots, as distinct to alphanumeric characters, but including "block graphics" made up of predefined shapes and patterns used like alphanumeric characters.

GRAPHICS TABLET. A flat-bed input device which can detect and transmit to the computer the position (co-ordinates) of a puck or stylus moved over its surface. They are mostly used for CAD, but can be used for d.t.p., as an alternative to a mouse. Formerly frequently called digitisers, this term is not much now used as it causes confusion with scanners, also sometimes called digitisers.

GRID. A system of regularly-spaced lines (visible or invisible) on the computer screen, to which the cursor can be made to "snap". They are used to simplify alignment and accurate drawing, and also the placing of text columns, etc.

GUTTER. The space between text columns. The fold between pages.

HALF-TITLE. The first page of a book, to which the front endpaper is usually attached. It can also mean any pages dividing sections within a document.

HALF-TONE. An illustration, especially photographs, broken up into dots of varying size for reproduction.

HANGING INDENT. Text, normally the first line of a paragraph, set beyond (to the left of) the left margin used for the remainder of the text.

HEAD. The top margin of a page.

HEADER. A running title printed in or just below the head of every page in a document, e.g., carrying the book title or chapter number.

HOT METAL. A form of typesetting formerly used in newspaper, books and magazine production. Now virtually obsolete.

ICON. A small symbol representing a computer operation, either on the screen or on a graphics tablet menu. Normally selected by "pointing and clicking" with the mouse or stylus.

IMPOSITION. The arrangement of pages on a printing plate, so that they are in correct sequence when the printed sheet is folded and trimmed.

IMPRINT. Printed copyright information. Printed bibliographical information. The publisher's name or trademark.

INDENT. Space left between the left margin and the left end of a text line, commonly used at the start of each paragraph.

INFERIOR FIGURES. Subscripts. Small figures printed below the baseline.

INITIAL LETTER. A single, large letter used at the beginning of a story, section or paragraph.

ITALIC. The sloped or oblique version of a typeface, with letter forms based on handwritten rather than engraved forms.

JUSTIFICATION. The action of fitting text to a margin or margins. Text may be left-justified, right-justified, or both, or unjustified. Where text is justified to both margins, extra space is inserted between words and letters to pad lines out to the required length.

KERN. A part of a character which overhangs another character to avoid the appearance of excessive spacing.

KERNING. Adjusting the spacing between characters. In particular, reducing the spaces between adjacent characters with sloping sides (e.g. AW) to improve the appearance.

KERNING TABLE. A table giving recommended amounts by which the space between certain pairs of characters should be adjusted in a particular font.

LAID PAPER. Paper made by a method which leaves a pattern of lines visible when the paper is held up to the light. The lines originate from the wires in the papermaking mould.

LANDSCAPE. A common description for a document which is wider than it is high. Photographs or other illustrations which are wider than high are also described as "landscape format", as opposed to "portrait format".

LASER PRINTER. A type of printer much used for d.t.p. which uses photocopier technology to print on paper. Laser printers offer high print quality (though matched now by some inkjet printers) and reasonable speed, especially when several copies of each page are required. Laser printers are expensive, and also rather large and heavy.

LAYOUT. The arrangement of text, illustrations, decorative features and white space on a page.

LEADERS. Lines of dots or other characters, such as dashes, used to lead the eye across the page from one piece of text to another. They are, for instance, frequently used between the chapter names and the corresponding page number on contents pages.

LEADING. (Pronounced like the metal lead.) The amount of vertical space between one line of text and the next. It is normally expressed in points, including the height of the text. Set text may be described, for instance, as "10 on 12-point", meaning that the characters are 10-point and the leading is 12 points.

LETTER SPACING. The spacing between letters. The use of this term normally implies that the spacing has been made wider than normal, to stretch the length of a line of text to fit the margins (see *justification*).

LINE FEED. 1. The spacing between lines of text, similar to leading. 2. The ASCII LF character, OA in hexadecimal notation, decimal 12.

LINE DRAWING (or line illustration). A drawing made up entirely of lines and solid areas without any graded half-tones, i.e. pure black and white.

LOGICAL DISK DRIVE. When you can address a single physical disk drive as if it were actually two or more drives (i.e. using two or more identifying letters or numbers), it is being used as two or more logical drives. For example, machines with a single floppy drive can frequently address this as either drive A or drive B. This is done largely to ease disk copying. You are prompted to change disks as necessary. A hard disk can also be partitioned into two or more logical drives. This is sometimes done to reduce access times, but it is also necessary with hard disks larger than 32 Mbytes with many versions of DOS.

LOGO (Logotype). A name or word in a specific style of lettering and design, used as a trademark. The term "Logo" is also frequently used to describe a company symbol (like the British Rail arrows), but strictly speaking this is incorrect.

LOWER CASE. The small letters in a font of type. The term comes from the days when the metal characters were stored in wooden cases. The capital letters were stored in the "upper case" and the small letters in the "lower case".

MACRO. In computing, a macro is usually a sequence of program instructions which can be recorded and stored (normally as a disk file) and subsequently executed as a single instruction. Frequently-performed operations can be automated in this way. (For example, we have a macro in our word processor which will mark the address in a letter as a block, and then send this block to the printer, formatted to print the envelope.)

MARGIN. The area between the text and any edge of the page (but, strictly, not the space between columns of text).

MATHS CO-PROCESSOR. An additional chip which can be installed in many computers. It works in close conjunction with the main CPU chip, and speeds up the performance of floating point maths by a factor of some hundreds. Software has to be written to use the co-processor, and it is only of advantage with programs which perform extensive floating point maths. A co-processor is unlikely to speed up the performance of a d.t.p. program very much, even if it is capable of using one. It can be a great advantage with graphics programs, especially of the CAD type, which normally can use such a chip (in fact, some CAD programs will *only* work if a co-processor is fitted).

MEASURE. The width of a column of text.

MECHANICALS. The American term for artwork.

NEWSPRINT. A very cheap quality of paper, made from unrefined wood pulp. It is only intended for newspapers and similar ephemera, as it will yellow and deteriorate quickly.

OPACITY. The degree to which you can "see through" paper. A paper with high opacity is desirable if it is to be printed on both sides.

OUTLINE CHARACTER. A character which is drawn in outline only, and not filled in. Some d.t.p. programs can generate outline characters from standard fonts. They are mainly used for headlines and decorative features.

OUTLINE FONT. Generally, a font in computer-readable form in which each character is described as a series of lines and curves, without reference to actual size. Fonts of any size (within the limits of the program) can be generated from the outlines, either by the d.t.p. program, a font generator program, or by the printer.

PAGE. One side of a leaf.

PAGING. Dividing the text and illustrations comprising a document into pages. Dividing galley proofs into pages.

PAGE DEPTH. The vertical height of the text area on a page.

PARENTHESES. The standard "round brackets", ( ).

PASTE-UP. Type proofs and illustrations made up into a page by cutting up and sticking down onto a carrier sheet, as a guide.

PEN PLOTTER. An output device, a form of printer, which draws lines by moving a pen across the paper, which may either be flat or on a drum. Mostly used for CAD, they are not really applicable to d.t.p.

PERFECT BINDING. A method of binding a book by sticking the single pages together with an adhesive at the spine.

PICA. A typographical measure equal to 12 points (approx. one-sixth of an inch).

PIXELS. Picture Elements. The individual points on a computer screen. The individual dots making up a digitised image when in visible form.

POINT. The unit of typographical measure, approximately equal to 1/72 inch.

PORTRAIT. A document which is higher than it is wide (see *landscape*).

PROOF. Any test printing. A test printing to be checked for mistakes.

PROOF READER. A person who checks proofs, especially for spelling and grammatical errors.

QWERTY. A keyboard with the keys arranged in the traditional typewriter layout (from the first six keys on the second row down – the top row carrying the numerals).

QUARTO. A page a quarter the size of the full sheet. A sheet folded in four after printing.

QUOTES. Punctuation marks indicating speech or quotations. Single or double inverted commas.

RANGE (left/right). This means aligning text to the left or right margin respectively, with the other margin being left unjustified.

RASTER. The pattern of horizontal lines making up the computer screen image. The term Raster Graphics is used in CAD to describe graphics built up using this system, as opposed to Vector Graphics, where the CRT beam is directed around the screen to describe the lines and curves of the image.

RECTO. The right-hand page of a two-page spread. Conventionally, the recto pages have the odd page numbers, and chapters always start on a recto page.

REGISTER. This refers to the exact positioning of two or more printings on a sheet. It is especially used in colour printing, to express how well the four or more colours making up the full-colour image are aligned. If they are "out of register", colour fringing can be seen.

REGISTER MARKS. Special marks, normally crosses within cricles, which are used to enable the printer to ensure correct registration in printing. They are normally placed on part of the sheet which will be trimmed off or hidden in the bound document.

RESOLUTION. The fineness of detail which can be reproduced by a printer, normally expressed in dots per inch. Dot matrix printers can normally print 120–180 dots per inch, laser printers 300–600 d.p.i., and phototypesetters from 1200 d.p.i. upwards. Also used to express the amount of detail a scanner can record when digitising an image, also expressed in dots per inch. Metrication is making slow progress in this area.

REVERSING OUT. Printing white text on a black or shaded background.

RING BINDER. A binder for sheets of paper which passes metal rings through holes punched in one edge of the sheets. Normally used for documents where pages may be added or changed ("loose-leaf" documents).

ROMAN FIGURES. Figures made up from the characters I, V, X, C, M as opposed to Arabic figures.

RULES. Lines of various thicknesses, including dotted and dashed lines, and multiple lines, used as dividers, boxes, and decorations.

RUN. The number of copies of a document to be printed in a print run.

RUN ON. Extra copies printed over and above the intended number in a print run. Also used in typesetting to mean text continuing on the same line.

RUNNING HEAD(ER)/FOOTER. Text printed at the head or foot of every page of a document (may be omitted on blank pages or the first pages of chapters, etc.).

SADDLE-STITCH. A method of binding where the document is held together by a wire or thread sewn through the centre of a folded section.

SANS SERIF (SANSERIF). Descriptive of a plain typeface, without decorative serifs (e.g. Helvetica, Univers, Futura).

SECTION. A single printed sheet, folded to page size, also called a *folded section.*

SELF-COVER. A cover to a document which is made of the same type of paper as the rest of the document.

SEMI-BOLD. A typeface weight between normal and bold.

SERIF. The small decorative strokes and features at the ends of the main strokes of letters.

SERIFIED. Descriptive of a typeface which has serifs.

SET SOLID. Type set without extra space between the lines.

SHOW-THROUGH. This is when printing on one side of a page can be seen from the reverse side.

SIDE-HEADING. A subheading placed in the margin.

SLAVE FILE. A temporary file, on disk or in RAM disk, used to hold data generated by a program, and normally deleted when the program is properly executed. Many d.t.p. programs generate very large slave files, and therefore may need a fair amount of free disk space to operate correctly.

SMALL CAPS. Letters of capital form, but the height of a lower case x.

SNAP. The ability of a program to move the cursor to predefined fixed points on the screen, but not to any point between them. Used to simplify accurate drawing (see *grid*).

SPINE. The bound edge of a document.

SPREAD. A pair of facing pages. A "two-page spread" is a layout which treats the two pages of a spread as a single entity for design purposes.

STRESS. The apparent slant of a letter, from vertical to oblique.

STYLE SHEET. In d.t.p., usually a file containing a basic page layout with text column guides, etc., and also perhaps headers and footers, paragraph styles, and font width files. The information which can be included in style sheets varies from program to program. Most d.t.p. programs come with some pre-defined style sheets, and users can modify these or design their own from scratch.

SUBHEADING. A heading within the body text of a document.

SUPERIOR FIGURES. Small figures placed high in the line of text. Superscripted figures.

TABLOID. A page half the size of a broadsheet. A newspaper which appeals to a "middling and inferior" readership.

TAPE STREAMER. A device which can copy the entire contents of a hard disk onto a tape cartridge for backup purposes.

TINT. An even tone made up of fine dots or lines, frequently as a background to headings.

TITLE PAGE. The page which gives the title of the work and the name of the author and publisher. It is normally the first or third page in a document.

TONE. The strength of a colour of shading, from solid to light, often expressed as a percentage.

TRANSPARENT. 1. A background tint to a text block or graphic which allows anything underneath the material to show through. 2. A computer operation which is performed automatically without the user needing to perform any action, or being aware that it is happening.

TRIMMED SIZE. The final size of a document when cut into pages.

TYPEFACE. The design of a set of characters comprising a font. The aspect of a letter form which has been designed.

TYPESCRIPT. Copy prepared on a typewriter, as opposed to a *manuscript*, which strictly means a hand-written document. Presumably text prepared on a word-processor is a wpscript!

TYPESETTING. Preparing text in some form, such that it can be printed by some method.

ULTRA (-BOLD). A typeface of a weight heavier than bold.

UNJUSTIFIED. Text which is aligned to the left margin but left ragged on the right margin. Left-ranged text.

UPPER CASE. Capital letters. See "lower case" for an explanation.

VERSO. The left-hand page of a two-page spread, or the reverse side of a single-page document.

WATERMARK. An identifying mark included in paper during manufacture, visible when a paper is held up to the light. It is normally only the better qualities of paper which are watermarked.

WEIGHT. Of typefaces, the degree of boldness of the typeface, ranging from extra-light to ultra-bold. Of paper, a measure of the thickness of the paper, expressed usually in grams per square metre (gsm) or pounds per ream.

WHITE SPACE. The blank areas on a page around the text and illustrations.

WIDOW. The last line of a paragraph appearing on its own at the top of a page.

WINDOW. A limited active area on the computer screen. Many computers allow multiple windows on the screen at one time.

Index